500 GUITARS

A QUANTUM BOOK

This edition published in 2010 by
CHARTWELL BOOKS, INC.
a division of BOOK SALES, INC.
276 Fifth Avenue Suite 206
New York, New York 10001
USA

QUMGUITA

ISBN-13: 978-0-7858-2618-7
ISBN-10: 0-7858-2618-1

This book is produced by
Quantum Publishing Ltd
6 Blundell Street
London N7 9BH

Publisher: Anastasia Cavouras
Project Editor: Valeria Kogan
Production: Rohana Yusof

Printed and bound in Singapore by Star Standard Industries (Pte) Ltd

500 GUITARS

CHARTWELL
BOOKS, INC.

Contents

Introduction

The guitar is an instrument that we all know; a box with the strings. It is almost a mundane aspect of our everyday lives that we think we completely understand: its music is piped in shopping malls and we see rockstars and models posing with them every day. We have it neatly pigeon-holed in our minds. But where did this stringed wonder come from, and what makes it so enduringly popular?

The guitar has its roots in the lute of Mesopotamia some 5,000 years ago. Ever since then, long and short-necked stringed instruments have been created within different cultures throughout history: the ancient Egyptian lute of the 18th Dynasty; the Roman cithara from 40AD; the Scandinavian 6-string lut circa 800AD; 11th Century Moorish and Latin guitars; and the 15th and 16th Century Spanish vihuela.

However, it was in the 15th and 16th Centuries with the advent of the baroque guitar in Europe that we see an instrument that is a recognizably close relation of the modern classical guitar.

While the history of the guitar could be said to be complicated and convoluted, if we take a look at the instrument today and try to summarize its qualities and characteristics we find ourselves looking at something of equal complexity.

To begin, how do we define a guitar?

Many might say something broadly along the lines of, "It is a wooden-bodied musical instrument with a fretted neck and six strings which are plucked or strummed with the fingers or a plectrum."

That description might adequately describe a good proportion of guitars, but what about those with more or less than six strings? Or guitars made from plastics, or metals such as aluminium and steel, and those made from high-tech materials like carbon graphite?

What about bass guitars? What about guitars and basses without frets? And guitars such as the Gittler that does not even have a neck, or the Teuffel Birdfish that does not have a body? What about pedal steel guitars? What about guitars that aren't plucked or strummed with the fingers or plectrum but are played using a tapping technique or are bowed or use electronic sustain circuitry?

Nearly every part of that simple definition of the guitar has its exceptions. In fact the only constant factor would seem to be that they are all musical instruments with strings, but even that fact is challenged by certain MIDI guitar-controllers.

All this diversity has to be what makes the guitar so special. As a musical instrument it can be exactly what we want it to be. We can add strings, subtract strings, add sympathetic strings, change tunings, use different construction techniques and materials to alter the tone, use different pickups, effects, or electronics... There is so much we can do with it.

This book aims to show you a cross-section of all these instruments, from early 15th and 16th Century baroque guitars through to popular iconic guitars such as the Fender Stratocaster and Gibson Les Paul and beyond to high-tech, cutting edge instruments such as The Handle from XOX Audio Tools. Along the way we'll look at resonator guitars, harp guitars, lap steel guitars, pedal steel guitars, and of course, bass guitars.

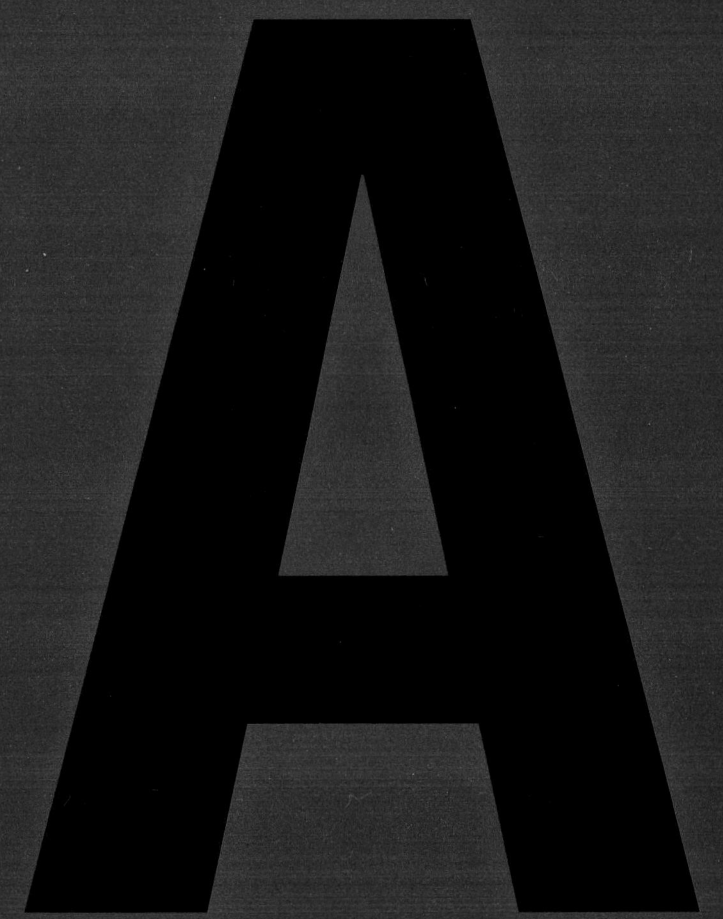

Abel Axe

Designed by Jeff Abel, the Abel Axe first made its appearance in the mid 1990s when the combination of its sustain-drenched tone and distinctive good looks made it instantly popular with hair metal bands, shredders and the occasional jazzer. The guitar featured a small Strat-like body made from a single piece of T6 aluminum billet, which was quite literally filled with holes. The holes were not just for aesthetic purposes; they had the much more important purpose of reducing the weight. A Kahler tremolo-equipped Abel Axe weighs in at approximately 9.5lbs; without the holes this would have been considerably more. (pictured opposite and on p11)

Abstract Gladiator

The Abstract Gladiator is not a guitar for shrinking violets or for the guitarist who wants to stand quietly at the back and keep well out of the limelight. Featuring a body that looks like it was modeled after a Klingon warrior's weapon and a head that reflects this same shape, you can guarantee that this USA-built guitar was built to appeal to shock rockers and metallers. Each guitar is custom-made so the guitarist can choose a body made from one of a whole range of exotic tonewoods. Other options include headless with Steinberger or Floyd Rose Speedloader trem.

Acoustic Control Corporation Black Widow

Acoustic, well known for its range of instrument amplifiers, produced the Black Widow guitar in the early 1970s. The symmetrical twin-cutaway carved-top design was created by former Rickenbacker, Magnatone and National employee Paul Barth. Most were built in either the Matsumoto Moko or Hoshino factories in Matsumoto, Japan, but a very small quantity of later examples were built by Mosrite in the USA and are therefore much sought after by collectors. To muddy the story even further, earlier hollow-bodied Black Widow guitars and (mainly fretless) basses had been produced by Barth's own Bartell company (but confusingly appeared under the Hohner brand) in the late 1960s. Photographic evidence shows Jimi Hendrix playing a left-handed model in the studio while jazz guitarist Larry Coryell frequently played the Acoustic-branded version.

Seymour Duncan
Seymour Duncan

Adamovic Jupiter Hollowbody 6-string Bass

The Jupiter is a custom-built small-bodied modern singlecut styled bass. The neck/body join is ergonomically sculpted away at the back to remove mass and aid playability and playing comfort. The compact design and ergonomic shaping of this instrument is of benefit to bassists who suffer from repetitive strain injury or back pain. The hollow body is made of western red cedar topped and backed by flamed birch, while the neck is made of laminates of wenge and hard maple. The scale length is medium at 32". Pickups are by Heaussel and have pau ferro covers and other hardware includes Hipshot tuners and bridge.

Airline 59 Custom 2P

This distinctive Airline guitar will be instantly recognizable to many as the favored guitar of Jack White of the White Stripes. The originals were made from 1958 to1968 by VALCO, who also built guitars for the Supro and National brands. The bodies were made from Res-O-Glas, which was essentially fiberglass. In 2004 Eastwood Guitars started producing a new version of these Airline guitars alongside other retro-style guitars. This time the bodies were made of chambered mahogany but still kept the unusual rubber binding which, on the originals, served to hide the join between the front and back pieces of fiberglass.

Seymour Duncan
Seymour Duncan

Agile Intrepid Standard 828 8-string

8-string guitars often fall into the realm of custom-built instruments. After the successful integration of the 7-string guitar into the arsenal of many guitarists, some wanted to extend their sonic range further. The Agile Intrepid 8-string Standard offers a cost-effective solution for the guitarist wanting to experiment without having to spend a fortune. The guitar has a scale-length of 28.625 and so should be capable of descending well into down-tuned territories without any problems. Electronics-wise, the guitar features a simple set-up of a single Cepheus Alpha pickup and a volume tone, although the control cavity has been routed large enough for guitarists to be able to customize their guitars by installing additional electronics.

Alembic Spectrum

The Spectrum was created as a sister to the Europa bass after musicians complained that the bass was overpowering their baritone. This beautiful instrument is contoured to fit your body so that the guitar isn't simply an instrument it's an extension of the musician. While the neck is carved out of clear rock maple and laminated with purpleheart for reinforcement, the body is covered in a variety of exotic woods for a truly unique guitar. (see picture opposite)

Alembic Stanley Clarke Signature Bass

For many years jazzman Stanley Clarke's favorite bass was the one he called the "Brown bass", an instrument he has now retired after having spent many years collecting the battle scars of life on the road. This was an Alembic Series I, which featured an active pickup system powered from an external power supply. Body woods vary with individual models, but on the Stanley Clarke Signature edition the body is made from mahogany with a walnut top and a through-neck of maple with two walnut pinstripes. Some models are fitted with LEDs in the fingerboard inlays.

Amfisound Arctic Kelo Routa

Amfisound is a guitar manufacturer from Finland and while this Routa model resembles other V or Rhoads-inspired guitars, the finish is really quite unusual. It looks almost like the guitar has been fashioned out of a piece of driftwood. The name "Kelo" refers to a certain kind of old and dried-out silver-grey tree that can be found in Scandinavian forests. The wood is actually alder but has been artificially aged to look like ancient kelo wood. The hardware and frets have also been distressed and blackened so as to fit in with the theme of well-worn instrument.

Alvarez FC7103BK

The FC1073 from Alvarez is an ultra-thin chamber-bodied folk guitar. The back and sides are made of mahogany while the top is made out of select spruce. The guitar's top lacks a soundhole as it is specifically intended for use in amplified performances since having a thin body has little acoustic projection of its own. It is fitted with Fishman AURA IC electronics, which provide a range of authentic-sounding acoustic tones while the thin body makes the guitar a good choice for long gigs.

American Showster 57 Chevy

Originally appearing in the late 1980s, the American Showster 57 Chevy guitar certainly has a distinctive look. Designed to resemble the tailfin of a Chevrolet car, the guitar incorporates lashings of chrome and comes complete with an operational brake-light. The guitars were available with optional custom graphics and a bass model was also available. Originally these guitars were built in Bayville, NJ, but from 1997 a Standard Series was produced in the Czech Republic and Slovakia. The company also made a guitar model featuring a body resembling a motorcycle gas tank. Showster also collaborated with Kramer to build a collection of more traditional guitars featuring thin metal bodies. (see picture opposite)

Ampeg AUB-1 Bass

The curvaceous body of the fretless AUB-1 and fretted AEB-1 scroll-headed bass has a pair of decorative f-holes passing through it. Strings are anchored at a tailpiece extending beyond the base of the body to facilitate the necessary string angle over a “mystery” pickup in early models. The pickup was essentially a steel diaphragm over two magnetic coils set in epoxy, enabling the use of gut strings. In a further attempt to appeal to upright bass players, a spike could be fitted allowing the bass to be played in the upright position. The models fitted with magnetic pickups and steel strings achieved more popularity than the original model. Debuting in 1966, the AUB-1 was possibly the first production model fretless bass.(see picture opposite)

Ampeg Dan Armstrong Plexiglass Guitar

Released in 1969, Dan Armstrong guitars and basses looked nothing like their guitar predecessors; bodies were made of clear acrylic, a body material that looked amazing and produced a clear, even tone and excellent sustain. The body's deep cutaways provide access to the top of the 24-fret neck. For stability, the neck was set deep inside the body and hidden from the front by a Formica woodgrain-look pickguard. The location of the neck joint meant there was no room for a neck pickup, but Armstrong got around this by having interchangeable pickups with different tonal characteristics that could be easily slotted into the body and changed at will.

Andreas Black Shark

Built in Austria between 1995 and 2003, the Andreas Black Shark is so named for the shark-like fin at the rear of the body. This also has a practical advantage as the fin offers support to the player's right forearm. The body and neck are crafted out of maple while the 22-fret fingerboard and headstock are of aluminum. The guitar is fitted with Andreas pickups (or alternatively EMGs or Seymour Duncans depending on preference), Schaller graphite nut, locking tuners and bridge. A tremolo-equipped model was also available.

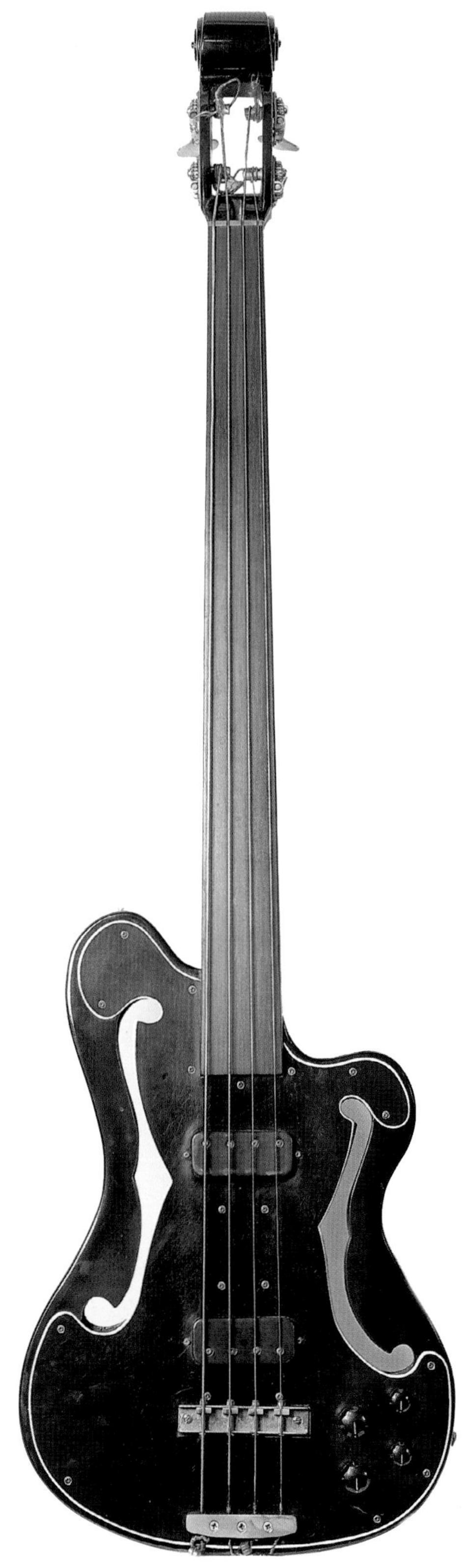

Aria SB1000 RI Bass

If you play bass in a 80s-era covers band then this is the bass for you! The Aria SB1000 was exceedingly popular in that decade, appearing in the hands of artists such as Duran Duran's John Taylor. The top is made of ash and the heelless through-neck is a 5-ply maple/walnut affair topped off with a 24-fret ebony fingerboard. The bass has a single MB-1E double coil pickup which when allied with the active tone circuitry allows for a wide range of tonal options. A version with passive electronics, the SB700, was also available. (see picture below)

Aria ZZ-2

Another 1980s-era guitar, the Aria ZZ-2, was quite obviously inspired by the Gibson Explorer although Aria made the design their own with a slimmer body with softly beveled edges. The guitar features a bolt-on maple neck shaped for comfort and speed with a rosewood fingerboard. The original 1980s version had an alder body which often featured thunderbolt-style graphics. The ZZ series was produced by Aria from 1982 to 1986 but didn't reappear until it was re-launched with some cosmetic differences in 2004. Other Z-shaped Arias appeared in the interim, and the same factory produced what was essentially the same guitar for other brands, only allowing subtle variations in the headstock. (see picture opposite)

Art & Lutherie
Canada

Art & Lutherie Ami

Art & Lutherie guitars are handcrafted in the small town of Princeville, Quebec, using 95% Canadian woods. The wood is gathered in eco-friendly fashion from fallen trees in Eastern Canada's forests. The Ami is A&L's re-creation of a 1900s-era parlor guitar; a small-bodied acoustic which, in recent years, has been coming back into favor, achieving particular popularity with fingerpickers or those who want a more compact guitar. The neck meets the body at the 12th fret instead of the more modern 14th fret join - some would argue that this allows for better tonality from a guitar of this size. The guitar is also available in a nylon-strung classical version.

Ashbory Bass

The history of the Ashbory bass is a confusing one as, over the years, it has been through several different incarnations and has been produced by different manufacturers including Guild and DeArmond (now owned by Fender). Designed by Alun Ashworth-Jones and Nigel Thornbory, the Ashbory is a diminutive 18"-scale electric bass fitted with silicon rubber strings. As it uses a piezo-transducer pickup, the Ashbury bass captures a sound that is often likened to that of a plucked double bass. It's not an overly popular instrument for live work - mainly because it looks like a toy - but it is taken more seriously as an instrument in the studio because of the immense sound it can produce.

Atlas Custom Guitars Uranus

Atlas has been hand-crafting guitars since 1962 and its aim is to provide an impeccable product at an affordable price. The highly sculpted Uranus is perhaps its most unusual looking model. The spiky design is possibly a homage to BC Rich, while the money-grip "handle" in the body is an idea we have also seen executed on Ibanez Jem series guitars. The body is made from alder with a curly ash top, the neck is maple, the fingerboard ebony with abalone lightning inlays, and the guitar is equipped with two hand-wound humbuckers, Floyd Rose tremolo and locking nut.

Auerswald Instruments Model C

This is one of the most eccentric looking guitar designs ever. It features a bar connecting the body to the headstock on the treble side of the instrument and a cutaway at the top of the neck on the bass side of the body which actually goes beneath the strings. If you were shown a silhouette of this design you'd be hard pressed to guess that it was a guitar. It's only the presence of pickups and strings that gives it away. The headstock is devoid of tuners; tuning duties would appear to take place at the bridge end. Auerswald's most famous endorsee is Prince who has his own signature symbol-shaped guitar.

AV Basses 3-string

AV Basses are custom made in the Czech Republic and specialize in high quality one-off instruments. Many of the examples produced have 4, 5, 6 or even 7 strings, but for one particular customer all that was required were 3 strings. The bass features an alder body of eye-catching asymmetrical design with a scrolled upper horn and is finished in high-gloss metallic green polyester. The 35" scale neck is a 7-piece lamination of ovangkol and maple and has a maple fingerboard with 24-frets. The bass has two Kent Armstrong Neo pickups and chrome Gotoh hardware including individual minibridges for each of the three strings.

Azahar 140 Classical

Azahar produce a range of quality value-priced instruments in Spanish and classical guitar styles. The 140 Classical guitar features a soundboard of massive cedar, while the back and sides are made of rosewood. Cedar is again used for the neck and the fingerboard is rosewood. The bridge and binding are also made of rosewood. While the guitar is in the entry-level price range, it is made with professional construction and has the same level of playability. The guitar is made in Mexico and makes an excellent starter instrument for someone wanting to take up classical guitar.

Gene Autry Cowboy Guitar

Gene Autry was the singing cowboy on radio, TV and in the movies from 1930 to his retirement from performing in 1964. Over the years various Gene Autry cowboy guitars have been made available, from children's plastic toys through to real instruments of varying sizes. A typical example would be a parlor guitar; 12 frets to the neck body join and a garish illustration on the top showing Autry on horseback whirling a lasso over his head. Such cowboy guitars were often novelty items rather than quality playable instruments but have been the inspiration for tongue-in-cheek guitars such as Gretsch's "Way Out West", "The Showdown", "Sundown Serenade" and "Wild West Sweethearts" guitars. (see picture of the Gene Autry above)

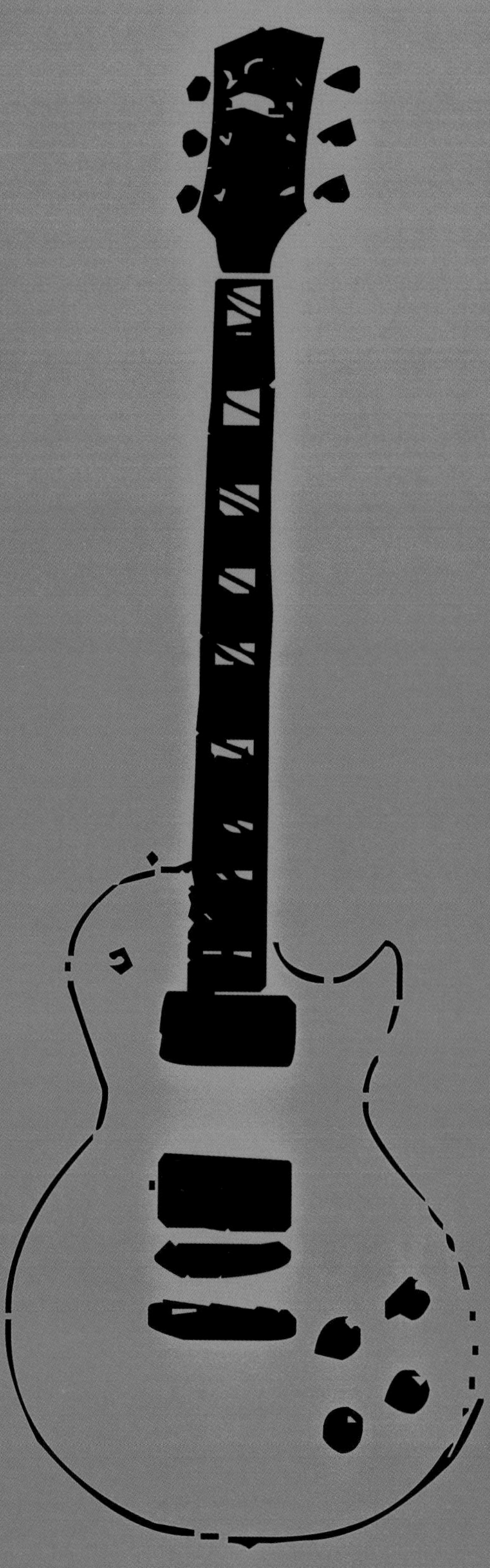

Babicz Indentity Series "Spider"

Babicz acoustic guitars feature an innovation they call the "lateral compression soundboard". Strings are not anchored at the bridge. Instead they pass under a bar behind the bridge and radiate out in an arc to six individual posts. This design apparently energizes the soundboard and dispenses with the stress that would normally be centered beneath the bridge. This means that the guitar does not need the heavy X-bracing found on many guitars and instead utilizes a more delicate bracing pattern. The top of the guitar is also much less taut than it would be with a standard bridge and thus the bass reproduction is better defined.

Barker Vertical Bass

The Barker Vertical Bass was designed by Lee Barker who found that playing bass in two bands each week was taking its toll on him and that, in particular, his wrists hurt. Experimenting with a bass of his own design he noticed that his wrists no longer hurt when playing an upright instrument. Unlike other electric uprights, the Barker bass is available in fretted and fretless versions and has the 34" scale familiar to most bass guitar players. It also uses regular Jazz Bass-style pickups. The bass is played on a stand, meaning that those suffering from bad backs will benefit. (see picture opposite)

BC Glass Studios

Brian Chivers of BC Glass Studio of Weukesha, Wisconsin, makes guitars out of fused glass. To begin with these were glass replicas for display purposes only, but a fellow Weukesha native, the legendary guitar innovator Les Paul, challenged him to "build one you can play". Chivers rose to the challenge and after much experimentation produced a playable guitar based loosely on the styling of the Les Paul guitar with the difference that,apart from its hardware and strings, this one was entirely made from fused glass.

BC Rich Bich 10-string guitar

The BC Rich Bich 10-string guitar was originally a custom-order handcrafted instrument, but in 2007 it was added to the Exotic Classic Series product line. The guitar functions in a similar way to a 12-string guitar although it lacks octave strings for the two lowest strings, which apparently allows the player to get a distorted tone without confusing and canceling the signal. The six regular guitar strings are tuned at the headstock while the four octave strings are tuned at machine heads in a cutaway at the rear of the body. The guitar has been used by Ric Ocasek of The Cars, Slash and Joe Perry.

BC Rich Black Widow Bass

The BC Rich WMD Widow Bass has an angular, vaguely arachnid-shaped body which is no doubt designed to appeal to heavier rock and metal bands and the people who love them. The fact that Blackie Lawless of the metal band W.A.S.P designed it only adds to the appeal. The bass is of a neck-through construction; the body being fashioned out of nato (also known as eastern mahogany) while the neck is made of maple, that most solid of timbers. The ebony fretboard has 24 jumbo frets and the scale length is 35". For pickups the bass is equipped with an active EQ pair of P-style units.

BC Rich Mockingbird

There have been many different versions of the BC Rich Mockingbird guitar. One thing they all have in common is the same radically asymmetric shape. The Mockingbird was originally designed in 1974 by Johnny A Go Go, but didn't appear in the BC Rich catalogue until 1978 when Bernie Rico adjusted the design to correct the balance of the guitar. Early "Mockingbirds" are thus referred to as "Shorthorn" models, while post-1978 examples are Longhorns. The first bolt-on neck version appeared in 1980 under the Phoenix name, and in 1982 the tremolo-equipped Mockingbird 2 was launched. Famous players have included Slash, Joe Perry, Elliot Easton, Paul Gilbert and Roy Oribson.

BelAire MotorAve

The BelAire is a very cool-looking thinline semi guitar equipped with two TV Jones Filtertron or Wolftone Dr Vintage pickups and a Bigsby vibrato. The design seems to effortlessly marry together elements of Rickenbacker, Telecaster and Gretsch guitars while maintaining its own unique feel. The body is made of mahogany or Spanish cedar routed to leave a center core beneath the pickups and bridge. The neck is created from quartersawn mahogany and is scarf-ointed for strength and stability. Finish options are cherry, honey brown or "blacktop" nitrocellulose lacquer and are topped off with a brushed aluminum pickguard.

Bell Custom Guitars Jazzblaster

The Jazzblaster borrows the familiar Jazzmaster shape from Fender and adds an interesting twist of its own. The guitar features a set-neck mounted on a maple body with plexiglass wings. A mother-of-pearl pickguard adds that extra touch of class. Pickups are Amalfitani P90 units while the strings pass over a fixed bridge and through the body for increased sustain. As an optional extra, Bell guitars are available fitted with a super-bright LED illumination system. It's reminiscent of Rickenbacker's "Light Show" guitars although updated for the modern day.

Manuel Ballido Flamenco Guitar

Manuel Lopez Bellido was born in Granada in 1939, and apprenticed with Eduardo Ferrer. He is recognized throughout the world as one of the principal proponents of the Granada School of guitar building and has helped train many of its leading guitar makers. He is responsible for creating the guitars used by the world's very best flamenco players. With an annual output of between 20 to 25 guitars, Bellido lovingly handcrafts each using only traditional methods, the guitars themselves being inspired by those of Antonio Torres. Flamenco artists who have purchased his guitars are Juan Carmona "El Habichuela", Tomatito, and Manolo Brenes.

Beyond The Trees / Fred Carlson Sympitar

Inspired by instruments from other cultures such as the Indian sitar and the Norwegian Hardanger fiddle, Fred Carlson set about creating the Sympitar: a six-string acoustic guitar with a set of additional resonating strings. These sympathetic strings run in a channel inside the neck down to their own bridge set inside the top of the guitar. As on a sitar, this bridge is flat and causes the strings to buzz against it, flavoring the sound. The head of the guitar is enormous carrying 18 tuners - six for the regular guitar strings and 12 for the sympathetics. An access panel on the back of the guitar allows for internal adjustments. (see picture below)

Johann Willhelm Bindernagel Lyre Guitar, 1804

This lyre guitar by Johann Wilhelm Bindernagel of Gotha, Thuringia, Germany dates back to 1804. Such instruments were very much in vogue, particularly with wealthy young women, during the 1780s through to approximately 1810. However, the guitar's popularity waned with the availability of the mass-produced piano. Many lyre guitars had flat bases so that they could be stood upright in a prominent position and displayed proudly for all to see.

John Birch Superyob

The original silver-colored Superyob was built by English luthier John Birch for Dave Hill of Slade. Hill used it mainly for TV appearances as it tended to be neck heavy and its ray-gun shape didn't make it the most comfortable guitar to play in live situations. Eventually Hill tired of the guitar and sold it to a music shop where it was pounced upon and bought by Marco Pirroni of Adam & The Ants. Around this time it made a brief appearance in a promo video by Madness. Framus made a copy in orange around the time of the Slade in Flame movie, and in 2001 John Birch created Superyob 2 for Dave Hill, complete with LEDs in the neck and a laser.

Birdsong Guitars Cortobass

Short-scale basses were very popular in the 1960s and early 70s but soon fell out of favor as they were often very boomy and lacked mid and high tones. Built in Texas, the Cortobass by Birdsong Guitars has been designed as a professional short-scale bass with a big, rich tone. This mahogany-bodied bass has a 31" scale, is ergonomically designed for comfort, and weighing 7 to 8 pounds is ideal for the player of a smaller stature. A fretless version is also available as are other custom options.

BJ & Byrne Guitars Troubador

BJ & Byrne Guitars are built in a small workshop over a music shop in London's Denmark Street. Named after some of the best known rock venues in the UK, these guitars borrow design elements from some of the world's most famous guitars while retaining a character of their own. The mahogany-bodied Troubador has a shape that brings to mind a flipped-over Jazzmaster and is fitted with a 22 fret maple neck with rosewood fingerboard, Bare Knuckle pickups (hand wound in England) and a Bigsby vibrato.

Blackbird Rider Steel String

The Blackbird Rider is a compact-sized acoustic constructed entirely from carbon fiber, which not only makes the guitar virtually indestructible and lightweight but also allows for an ultra-thin soundboard. Despite its small paddle shape, the guitar offers a full 24.5" scale length. Its most unusual feature is its one-piece hollow-neck unibody that carries stereo soundholes - one on the upper bout of the body and the other in the guitar's head. A Fishman Matrix Infinity pickup system is optional. Blackbird also offers a nylon-strung version of this model plus a slightly more conventional full-size acoustic with similar features.

Black Machine B2

Black Machine guitars are built by luthier Doug Campbell in the UK, the design falling loosely into the "super-strat" category of twin-cutaway shred machines. The guitars are all built out of quality tonewoods such as various types of mahogany, Honduras rosewood or swamp ash with tops made of sapela or ebony. Rather than use conventional finishing methods, the guitars are oiled to bring out the beauty in the wood. They each feature neck-through construction and have exceedingly thin bodies; this results in an ultra-light guitar. Pickups are typically by Bareknuckle although the customer can specify their own preference.

Black Night CB-42

Living up to its name, the front of the Black Knight has a liquorice-black finish with a scalloped top and arrow-shaped headstock, but the back and sides are left in their natural maple state. The 24-fret rosewood fingerboard is pretty standard, but the real beauty of this guitar is revealed in the frontal contours, which reduce the need for the usual forearm and rib contours that would destroy the shape. Plastic covers hide the pole pieces of the two humbuckers to enhance the appearance of this menace.

Blackspot Guitars J2C Maple Turquoise

Patrick Alexander of Blackspot Guitars, based in Bristol, UK, builds a range of unique handmade instruments from ethically sourced timbers. Guitars are made from American Black Walnut, European Cherry or Canadian Maple and necks are set with a fully captive tenon joint. Fretboard position markers are of Blackspot's own distinctive circle, pickups are by Bareknuckle and other hardware is by Gotoh. The body shape looks something like a sucked lozenge with sharp corners – the design is highly individual meaning these guitars definitely won't get mistaken for anything else. Blackspot also produce a range of more conservative acoustics. (see picture opposite)

Blueberry Groove Classical

The Blueberry Groove guitar claims to be a historical acoustic breakthrough. Its entire cedar top is covered in hand-carved grooves laid out in panels. The mahogany back is similarly grooved. The pattern of these panels is not random; it has been carefully designed to enhance the guitar's acoustic properties and create a resonance beyond anything offered by other acoustic guitars of similar size. This model is the concert-sized guitar but reportedly has a similar resonance to that of a dreadnought.

Bohmann Harp Guitar, circa 1910-1915

There are many different kinds of harp guitar. Many are strange and cumbersome-looking instruments featuring body and head extensions or additional necks. Most have additional strings which can either function as sympathetic strings or be plucked as on a harp. The Bohmann Harp Guitar has 12 sympathetic strings on a separate fretless neck which merely acts as a support. The sympathetic strings are not meant to be played as such; their function is to resonate as the strings on the primary neck are played. The sympathetics can be muted using the damping bar, which has a push button alongside the bridge.

Bond Electraglide

The Bond Electraglide was the brainchild of Scotland's Andrew Bond. It was a one-piece carbon graphite construction and carried push-button activated on-board active electronics with a digital LED readout angled towards the player in the guitar's top. However, the biggest innovation was the "fretless" stepped-neck design of the carbon fiber fingerboard. This made for a very fast neck that could be played like a fretless while the stepped increments meant that it could also be played conventionally. However, many guitarists didn't like it because they found string-bending too awkward for regular play, but this did not stop Mick Jones, formerly of The Clash, from playing one in Big Audio Dynamite. (see picture left)

Born To Rock F4b Bass

The Born to Rock F4b bass is crafted from lightweight aluminum tube. The wooden neck is fronted with a 2-octave aluminum fretboard. The headless design means that the tuners are at the base of the instrument, preventing any neck heaviness. An interesting feature is the unique system replacing the traditionally used trussrod. The neck is suspended on pivots allowing the strings to position the neck. A string under tension defines a straight line; since the strings are straight, so is the neck. The sound is said to have incredible attack and overtones because of the open metal design.

Brazen Dynasty Vintage T

The Vintage T model from California's Brazen Guitars is inspired by the classic Tele shape and is equipped with 2 Alnico humbuckers, tune-o-matic bridge and traditional Bigsby vibrato for that vintage feel. The top of the alder body is carved with an attractive bevel and is finished with a bound edge that defines the body shape to perfection. The set-in neck is of maple and carries 22 frets on a 25" scale length. All in all, it makes for a guitar that looks familiar but unique with a vintage vibe.

Breedlove CM Custom

The Breedlove Guitar Company, based in Oregon, was formed in 1990 and builds many traditionally-styled acoustic guitars as well as basses and mandolins. The CM style guitar is a more radically shaped instrument of their own design, having an asymmetrical concert body with extra depth for increased bass response. The guitar features a western red cedar top with rosewood back and sides. The soundhole rosette is made of abalone and binding is grained ivoroid, and for an amplified sound the guitar employs the L.R. Baggs dual element pickup system: all these elements add to the exceptional sound of this instrument, complimented by stunning good looks. (see picture right)

Brooklyn Gear BG8 8-string Guitar

The Brooklyn Gear BG8 is a no-nonsense guitar for those wanting to play on 8-strings. The simple singlecut mahogany body pays respect to Gibson's Les Paul although with a much more restrained black finish and without any binding. Pickups are a pair of custom Tesla 8-string humbuckers and the bridge employs Monolithic bridge saddles for accurate intonation given the guitar's 27" scale length.

Brooklyn Gear KSD 6-string Bass

The Ken Smith designed 6-string bass from Brooklyn Gear takes the classic Fender Jazz Bass styling and adds a massive neck, which is wide enough for all 6strings with the regular string spacing across the neck that bass players are accustomed to. The bass features standard Jazz Bass appointments: two J pickups (albeit 6-string J pickups), volume controls for each and a single tone, and it is available in sunburst and ash finishes or as a fretless with a black finish.

Alfredo Bugari Stonehenge III

The Stonehenge guitar by Italy's Alfredo Bugari, who also built guitars for the Castelfidaro brand, is an odd-looking, triangular-shaped guitar that first appeared in 1984 but sank without trace shortly after its release. It has an open body formed by a tubular metal frame with minimal wooden inserts housing the DiMarzio pickups and electrics. The treble side of the body has a knee rest attached so the guitar can be played comfortably while sitting, (ask any Flying V player about difficulties playing when seated!). The Stonehenge has a very interesting design but is probably too radical for most guitarists.

Bunker Guitars TG2001

Bunker Guitars' TG2001 Touch Guitar is a strange-looking beast. It features two headless necks that are designed to be played simultaneously. The lower neck looks straightforward enough, being a 4-string bass (or, optionally, a 5-string bass). The top guitar neck is flat and wide and its strings pass beneath a wooden cover over the body. The concept is to play both necks touch style - the bass neck with the left hand in the usual position sounding notes by hammering on and tapping, and the top neck played with the right hand also using a tapping method. The wooden cover allows the right arm to rest over the body without dampening any strings. (see picture right)

Burns Bison

From possibly the best-known British guitar maker, Jim Burns – the UK's answer to Leo Fender - the Burns Bison made its debut in 1962, the heyday of instrumental guitar pop and beat music. The guitar, with its exaggerated curving horns, used an unusual scale length of 25", which sits midway between the scale lengths of Fender and Gibson. The Bison features Burns' own vibrato unit plus unique "Wild Dog" and "Split Sound" settings that allow the three high-output Burns Tri-sonic pickups to be selected in many different combinations. Present-day Bison players include Badly Drawn Boy and The Young Knives' Henry Dartnall.

Burns Flyte

Another of Jim Burns' creations, the Flyte, first appearing in 1977, is a supersonic-age instrument with a design inspired by the Concorde. Its pickups were specially designed by Burns to minimize feedback. These guitars were in vogue briefly with glam acts like T Rex and Slade and are highly sought after by collectors today, the silver finish often fading to a dull gold. Burns also produced The Mirage, which looked like a Flyte with its neck attached to the wrong end of the body. A far-eastern built Flyte has become available in more recent years in redesigned format with a treble-side cutaway. A bass version is also available.

Burns Jet Sonic

The Jet Sonic is a post-Jim Burns design, courtesy of Italian designer Pagelli. At first glance it looks like someone has taken a saw to a Les Paul but a closer inspection reveals some tasty curves and contours, and the gently curving upside-down 6 in-a-line head complements its weird good looks. Otherwise the layout is pretty standard fare, with two Burns split-coil humbuckers (albeit in parallelogram-shaped casings), single volume and tone and 3-way selector switch. The Jet Sonic is played by Justin Hawkins formerly of The Darkness.

Burns Scorpion Bass

The Scorpion Bass is aptly named as its inwardly curving horns - echoed by another pair at the rear of the body - bring to mind the pincers of a scorpion. The headstock additionally sports a small pair of pincers just to drive home the message: this machine bites! The Scorpion was introduced in 1979 and a modernized version is still in the Burns catalogue today. Early UK-built versions are easily recognizable thanks to the chrome rectangular plate that sits under the bridge and around the pickups. (see picture below)

Burrell Venture Class 24 Fret Acoustic

When you first lay eyes on a Burrell guitar you would be forgiven for thinking your eyes were deceiving you: the guitar appears to be all bent out of shape. In fact, these guitars are built to be highly ergonomic, to conform to the player's body and the natural movements of the hand as it moves around the fretboard. The Venture Class is unusual for an acoustic in having a full 2-octave fretboard. The back and sides are made of mahogany, the top is Kermodie spruce and the neck is curly maple. Note the offset headstock design with two tiers of three tuners both facing upwards towards the player.

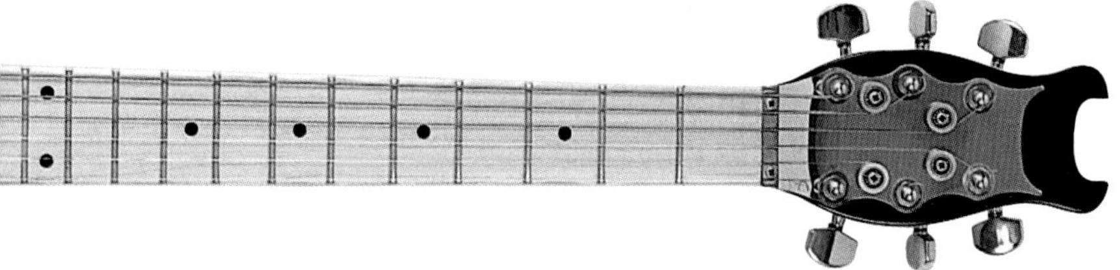

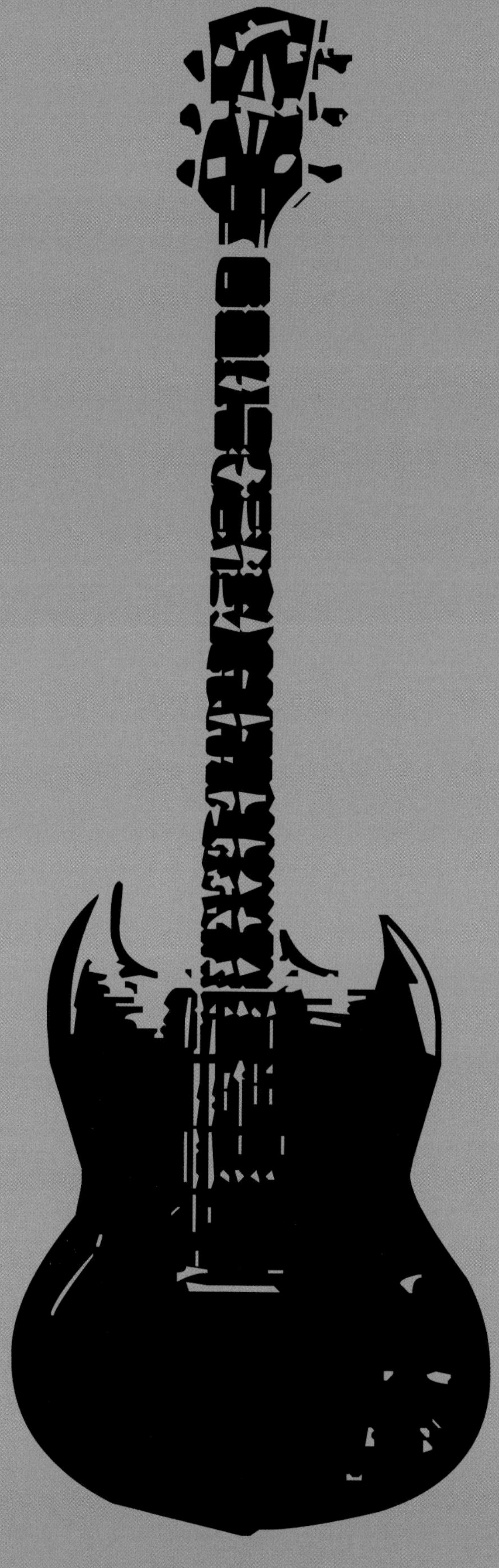

Cairnes
ENGLAND
COLT
CAIRNES
CAIRNES

Jim Cairns Colt Peacemaker Mark II

In the guitar world, the guitar shaped like a gun is a well-worn cliché, but if you're going to do it you may as well do it well. The Colt Peacemaker II guitar was made in England in 1970 by Jim Cairns, who also made pickups for Burns guitars; love it or loathe it, you cannot deny the attention to detail. For example, the hammer of the gun is the pickup selector, the trigger is the volume control, and the ejector rod is a push/pull tone control. The body is quite huge and judging by the amount of wood used plus the brass hardware, it must be one very heavy guitar.

Campbell American Guitars Nelsonic

The Nelsonic is the signature guitar of former Be-Bop Deluxe guitarist Bill Nelson and is handmade by Campbell Guitars in the Blackstone Valley, New England. The guitar is based on Campbell's own Transitone model although it has more of a retro 1950s atomic-age feel to it. The guitar is fitted with a pair of Seymour Duncan humbuckers, gold hardware and Gotoh roller bridge tremolo. The Honduran mahogany body is finished in Rocket Ship Red with nitrocellulose lacquer while the 22-fret ebony neck features two Red Sea Coral atom inlays at the 12th fret.

Canvas Guitars CVN20HH

The Canvas CVN20HH claims to be the first electric guitar designed specifically for the lead singer in a band. Using the somewhat shaky logic, since lead singers often play rhythm guitar on non-cutaway acoustics, the makers argue that they should also have a non-cutaway electric guitar. Nevertheless, this is a very attractive instrument. Constructed from mahogany with a spruce cap, it is lightweight like an acoustic. The neck is also made from mahogany, supposedly for an acoustic-like tone and better balance. The electrics of the guitar are comprised of two vintage-style Alnico5 humbuckers, 3-way switch plus master volume and tone controls.

Caparision Susanoh

Ace, of Japanese band Face To Ace, plays a Caparison Susanoh guitar, which is named after the Shinto god Susanoh's powerful storm of summer in Japanese mythology. The mahogany body has a flame maple archtop and is married to a mahogany neck with an ebony 24-fret fingerboard. The two single-coil and humbucker pickups are Caparison's own while the locking nut and tremolo are by Schaller. The controls are simple: master volume, 5-way switch, and two mini-toggles for coil tap and other pickup combinations. In appearance the guitar resembles a sharper version of Brian May's Red Special.

J.E. Carpenter Classical Cutaway

Besides working as a luthier, Jesse Carpenter has been extensively involved in woodworking, cabinet design and historic restoration for over thirty years. He was taught to play classical guitar in his high school years, and has returned to the guitar in his semi-retirement in the capacity of handcrafting them himself. He has bravely experimented with unusual-shaped instruments in this notoriously conservative field, and his designs have been known to feature such elements as off-center soundholes, deep cutaways and complex on-board electronics.

Charvel Surfcaster

The Surfcaster was something of a departure for Charvel when first released in 1992. Up until then most Charvel designs had been in the "superstrat" mold aimed firmly at the hard rock acts. The Surfcaster owed more to the stylings of Rickenbacker with its semi-hollow construction, cats-eye soundhole, body binding and sharkfin fingerboard inlays. The guitar also featured a pearloid pickguard and a pair of diagonally mounted lipstick tube pickups similar to those found on Danelectro guitars. With its clear, bell-like tone, vintage twang and curvaceous good looks it soon became a favorite with alternative genre acts, and players include Belinda Butcher of My Bloody Valentine, Mark Collins of The Charlatans and Scott Ian of Anthrax.

Charvel EVH Art Guitar

Eddie Van Halen's involvement with Charvel guitars goes back to when he put together his first guitar using an imperfect body and neck he'd bought from Wayne Charvel's guitar shop. Over the years Van Halen's distinctively striped "Frankenstrats" have spawned numerous replicas and tribute guitars. The EVH Art Series is a limited edition series of replicas of his most recognizable early guitars. Each guitar is built from Charvel parts and is hand striped and autographed by Eddie Van Halen himself and verified with a photograph of Eddie playing the guitar live. Surely, the ultimate guitar for the Van Halen fan!

Charvel Michael Angelo Quad-400

Michael Angelo Batio, Guitar One Magazine's "No1 Shredder of All Time" in 2003, is known for his unusual party-piece of playing on two necks at once on a specially-made double-necked guitar, with a right handed neck at one end and left-handed neck at the other. The Quad guitar is an extension of this concept - a four-necked guitar with two necks on either side. Wayne Charvel built the guitar - which is actually made up of four guitars that can be disassembled into individual units - for Batio. The top two necks have seven strings each while the lower two have six strings each.

Charvel San Dimas Style 1-2H

The Charvel San Dimas Style 1-2H is a USA-built production model based on the early Charvel San Dimas guitars from the period before Jackson Guitars took over ownership of the company. These guitars are essentially hot-rodded Strats made from high quality parts. Ironically, Charvel is now owned by Fender. The Style 1-2H features a one-piece maple neck with a compound radius of 12" to 16" on an alder body fitted with Seymour Duncan humbuckers, Floyd Rose tremolo and Grover mini tuners. The electrics are installed from the rear so there is no need for the usual Strat pickguard.

Chrysalis Guitars

The Chrysalis guitar is a modular acoustic guitar that can be assembled in minutes from component parts that pack into a small carry-anywhere case. The main structural elements that make up the body of the guitar are made from carbon graphite. The two halves of the body top, the neck, the headstock and the bridge all clip together while an inflatable body attaches to the back of the guitar to act as the acoustic soundbox. The guitar benefits from amplification, functioning at its best in electro-acoustic mode.

Clearport Summit Acoustic

The Clearport Summit is a dreadnought-shaped guitar crafted from rosewood with a spruce top. Viewed from the front the guitar appears to be made according to a double cutaway design, but if viewed from behind it is seen to be a non-cutaway acoustic. The "cutaways" are actually "Thurman multi-dimensional sound ports" designed to significantly increase the clarity and dynamic range of the guitar's natural acoustic tone by freeing the surplus energy inside the guitar. The ports also help project the sound forward to the listener and at the same time act as a monitor for the player.

Composite Acoustics Baritone

Handcrafted in the USA, the Composite Acoustics Baritone has a dreadnought acoustic body with a soundhole positioned towards the bass side of the neck. The rigid one-piece body and neck are created using composite construction, providing consistent action and playability. The guitar features a 28" scale suited to its baritone tuning. On-board electronics are courtesy of L.R. Baggs Stage Pro and include Volume, EQ, tuner and phase options. The guitar is said to be impervious to climatic changes and will not split or break, doesn't require a trussrod and allegedly stays in tune.

" I'm just a guitar player in a band that's doing really well right now."
- Slash

Clifford Essex Paragon De Luxe

Although few people would recognize a Clifford Essex Paragon De Luxe guitar if they saw it, they definitely would know what it sounds like. In the hands of guitarist Vic Flick, this is the guitar that originally played that most famous of guitar riffs in John Barry's "James Bond" theme. The guitar is a non-cutaway archtop jazzbox with a pickup mounted at the neck and a small unit carrying the volume and tone controls clipped to the bridge. The guitar currently resides in the Rock and Roll Hall of Fame and Museum in Cleveland, Ohio. (see picture below)

Coral Sitar

Strictly speaking not a true sitar, the Coral Sitar is an electric guitar fitted with a buzz bridge and a set of 13 sympathetic strings on the upper part of its body and is designed to emulate the sound of the traditional Indian instrument. It was developed in the late 1960s just in time for the advent of psychedelic music, which it was perfectly suited to. Coral Sitars were made by Danelectro and shared certain features with the guitars such as the masonite-on-a-pine-frame body construction and the lipstick tube pickups, of which the Coral had three - two for the guitar strings and one for the sympathetics.

Cort Pagelli

Designed by Claudio Pagelli, the Cort Pagelli is certainly a mean-looking electric guitar that is eminently suited to heavy rock. With its gorgeous curves and body contours, the guitar is based loosely on the classic singlecut shape with a few tweaks here and there. Selling at a budget price, you'd be forgiven for thinking this guitar was made of inferior materials, however the body is solid mahogany. It would be an excellent choice of instrument for the beginner, while the more experienced and discerning player might want to swap out the pickups for a set with a little more poke. (see picture of a cort larry opposite)

Crafter SA-BUB

The SA-BUB is Crafter's take on the hybrid acoustic/electric guitar, very possibly inspired by the likes of Taylor's T5 model. It is a thinline archtop, as might be guessed from its model designation. Its top is made from Bubinga and is pleasing to the eye. Rather than being a true acoustic, it is a solid with an acoustic sound chamber. To achieve a range of tones from acoustic to electric the player is able to blend and mix the output from a Kent Armstrong lipstick pickup and a L.R. Baggs Element pickup via an on-board preamp. (see picture opposite)

Crimson Guitars 05Ric Extended Range Bass

This instrument, a collaboration between Ben Crowe at Crimson Guitars and the extended-range bassist known as 05Ric, was two years in the making from concept through to design and construction. It is a 7-string bass built with ergonomics in mind. The maple-topped cedar body is shaped to provide forearm support and takes its inspiration from the Klein guitar. The through-neck is a multi-laminate of mahogany and maple, and the bridge sits on a section extending beyond the body, which provides a counterbalance to the headstock. Two powerful custom Wizard pickups are hidden beneath 8mm of solid rosewood.

Crimson Guitars Steve Evans Signature

Ben Crowe at Crimson Guitars in the UK built this beautiful guitar for Steve Evans, who has played guitar for Robert Plant and Siouxsie Sioux. The highly polished body has been hand-carved for ergonomic comfort from a block of rubean red perspex; proof that acrylic-bodied guitars do not have to be slab-bodied. The glued-in neck is a padouk and maple laminate, with a dual-action trussrod and a red perspex center-section in the headstock matching the body. The bridge is also fashioned from red acrylic, as are the control knobs. Pickups are transparent cast units by Wizard. (see picture below)

Ted Crocker Honey Dripper

Crocker guitars were chosen to create the rustic-looking guitar seen in 2007's "Honeydripper" movie directed by John Sayles. In the film, it is the first electric guitar to be seen in 1950s small town Alabama, the script describing it as "a neck screwed to a plank with strange wires". The actual guitar is designed to look period correct and features handmade hardware. The body is formed from a single piece of Honduras mahogany, with leopardwood used for other wooden parts. Note the three pickups, each for a pair of strings, the chickenhead volume knob, and the feather in the pickup cavity to add a little mojo.

Crucianelli Elite V2

In the early 1960s music boom the electric guitar was suddenly in great demand. In Europe many musical instrument manufacturers who had been producing accordions jumped onto the guitar bandwagon, leaving us a legacy of garish-looking guitars with pearloid or glitter finishes and with banks of pushbuttons. The Crucianelli V2 (sometimes called "Elite") is a "mother of pearl" vinyl-covered example from Italy, which is where some of the most outrageous-looking guitars came from. Beneath the vinyl the body is cheap plywood, and the guitar is equipped with a vibrato and a very restrained two pickups (in this era four pickups was not unusual).

Crystal Guitars The Starman

Jeff Star Saxon of Crystal Guitars in Detroit, Michigan, builds a range of custom guitars with transparent acrylic bodies. The Starman is one such model, with a see-through body design based on that of the Ibanez Iceman. The neck is made of maple with a rosewood fretboard, pickups are by Seymour Duncan, and each guitar has a holographic Crystal Guitars logo and glow-in-the-dark serial number. The tone is said to be clear and full of amazing resonance.

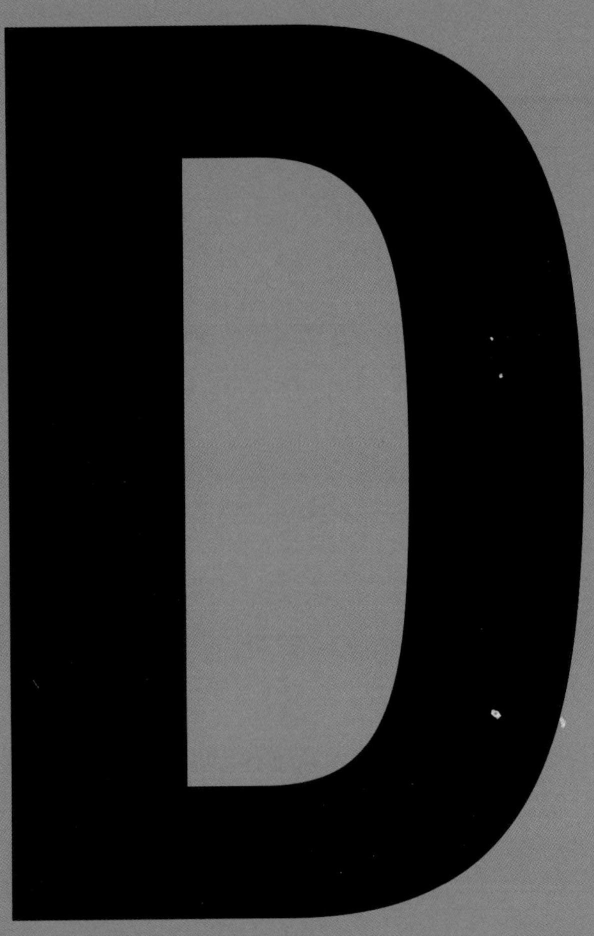

Daguet Guitars Proto Birdman

Daguet guitars are custom built in the South of France by R. Dag, who initially began making guitars as a hobby back in 1975. His guitars include Rickenbacker-inspired designs and some amazing Epiphone Crestwood replicas, whereas the Proto Birdman (named after Radio Birdman) is an original and very attractive design. It has a 24" scale, mahogany body with a maple top, mahogany through-neck and ebony fretboard. Pickups are three Seymour Duncan mini-humbuckers with two switches giving access to all available pickup combinations. Finally, the guitar is equipped with a Bigsby vibrato.

Daisy Rock Stardust Retro-H De-Luxe

Daisy Rock Guitars was founded in 2000 by Tish Ciravolo with an aim to making guitars for women and girls, a huge sector of the market that had been overlooked for too long by the major guitar manufacturers. The Stardust Retro-H De-Luxe is a small-bodied twin-cutaway thinline electric equipped with two mini humbuckers and Bigsby B-50 vibrato. The body is a semi-hollow basswood affair with a single f-hole in the upper bout, while the neck is rock maple with a 22-fret rosewood fingerboard. The end result is both retro and feminine at the same time without resorting to gratuitous cutesiness. (see picture on p60)

Daisy Rock Debutante Series Heartbreaker

With its heart-shaped body the Daisy Rock Heartbreaker does have that cutesy factor but nevertheless it is an aesthetically pleasing design. One of Dairy Rock's earlier models, this is one of a series of guitars aimed to appeal to younger female players. It features a short scale of 22", suitable for smaller hands. The layout is deliberately simple with a lone humbucking pickup and a single volume knob. The heart-shaped inlays in the rosewood fretboard provide a nice touch. (see picture opposite)

Debutante

Dallas Tuxedo

By today's standards, the late 1950s Dallas Tuxedo appears to be a rather primitive guitar. However, this unassuming little guitar has the distinction of being the first British solid electric, and is actually quite sophisticated in design with through-neck construction in solid mahogany. The guitar has a small narrow-waisted singlecut body and 19-fret neck with oversized head. One and two-pickup versions were both available, and the guitars carried a volume and tone control for each pickup. Some models also featured a Rangemaster tremolo. A young John Lennon is believed to have owned such a guitar.

Danelectro Convertible

Like most Danelectro designs the Convertible was constructed quickly and cheaply using unusual materials. The body was a pine frame sandwiched between front and back panels of masonite (hardboard). By all rights these guitars should have sounded dreadful, but the unusual construction coupled with the use of lipstick pickups gave them a unique resonance and a certain growl. The Convertible was an immensely popular model. Featuring a single lipstick pickup straddling a centre soundhole, it aimed to be both electric and acoustic in a single package. The unplugged sound was surprisingly loud but had a somewhat rattly quality.

Danelectro Longhorn Bass

The Danelectro Longhorn Bass shares the same basic construction as the Convertible. With a short-scale of 30" it is unusual in having a 24-fret neck with full access to the upper frets thanks to the deep cutaways in the lyre-shaped body. This, and its hollow resonant sound, makes the Longhorn a favorite with bassists. John Entwistle used one when The Who recorded "My Generation", although he was unhappy when he broke a string and had to overdub the solo with a Fender Jazz Bass, preferring the Danelectro's playability. Also, legend tells that because Longhorn strings were so hard to find Entwistle found it easier to buy a new Longhorn Bass each time he broke a string!

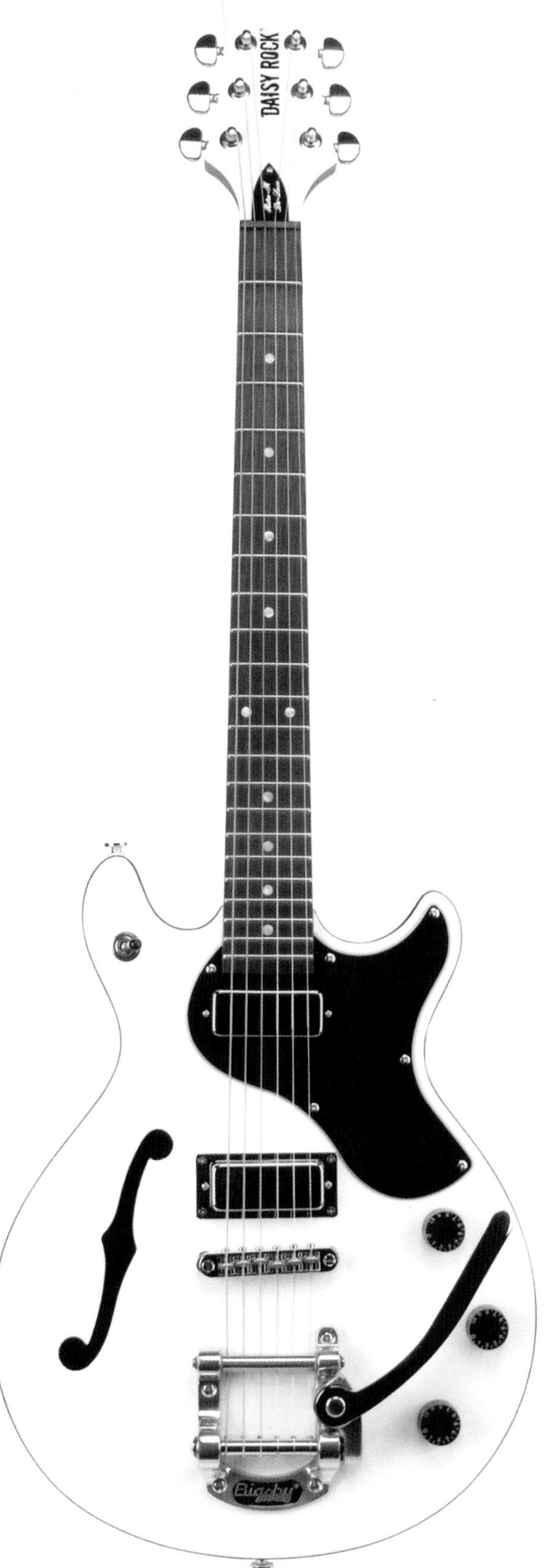
DAISY ROCK
Bigsby

D'Angelico New Yorker NY16

Born in 1905, John D'Angelico was a luthier in New York City specializing in archtop guitars and mandolins. He is believed to have hand built well over 1,000 guitars before his death in 1964. His guitars are some of the most highly rated by jazz guitarists. In more recent years the brand has been resurrected with guitars being manufactured in Korea. The NY16 has a 16" multi-bound arched body with solid mahogany back and solid figured maple carved top. Other features include polished brass stairstep tailpiece, ebony bridge, single humbucker and tortoise-style pickguard with volume/tone controls. This is a luxurious guitar in the D'Angelico tradition.

D'Angelico Excel

D'Angelico's guitar designs were constantly evolving. The Excel model dates back to 1934 when it was 16 5/8" wide with straight f-holes and engraved fingerboard inlays. By late 1937 the body had grown to 17" wide, and the f-holes were of the curved single-bound variety. Other features such as the multiple binding on top and back, block inlays and the highly ornamental headstock remained the same. From 1943 the "stairstep" tailpiece was introduced, and 1947 saw a major change when John D'Angelico introduced a cutaway to the design. Such cutaways are thought to have originated with Gibson's L-5 and Super 400 Premier models circa 1939.

D'Aquisto Centura

Jimmy D'Aquisto served as an apprentice to John D'Angelico in the early 1950s and went on to produce many fine archtop guitars in the same tradition. One of his most celebrated models is the "Centura", with originals fetching staggering sums in today's market. With its wide cats eye soundholes it was an innovative guitar, and was crafted from the most luxurious of woods: curly maple for the body and neck binding, Sitka spruce for the solid top, ebony for the fingerboard, narrow pickguard, bridge and tailpiece, and a gorgeous piece of Macassar ebony for the facing at the front and back of the headstock.

DBZ Guitars Imperial

DBZ Guitars was launched in 2008 by Dean B. Zelinsky after breaking away from Dean Guitars. With DBZ Guitars, Zelinsky plans to embrace modern technology to produce the next generation of guitars. The Imperial is crafted from mahogany with a maple top and set mahogany neck. From the front it looks like a big guitar, almost 335-ish in shape, but sideways on you can see this is one very slim-bodied guitar. Hardware is DBZ's own, with EMG pickups available as an option. The neck has the Z-diamond inlay at the 12-fret position, and a whole host of colors and finishes are available.

Dean Cadillac 1980

The Cadillac is an original design by Dean B. Zelinsky which dates back to 1980. The guitar looks like a composite of two classic Gibson guitars: part Les Paul, part Explorer. Like both those guitars, the Cadillac is designed with set-neck construction. It features a fully bound mahogany body and neck, and rosewood fingerboard with pearl block inlays. With two (or optionally three) humbuckers and a Les Paul-like control layout, this is a guitar sure to keep many a rocker very happy.

Dean Razorback Slime Bumblebee

The Dean Razorback Slime Bumblebee must surely be a contender for the guitar with the strangest name. It is one of a number of signature and tribute guitars produced by Dean for Damageplan guitarist Dimebag Darrell, who was tragically shot dead on stage in 2004. The Razorback guitar was designed by Darrell just months before his death. Essentially it is a modified, pointier version of the Dean ML model. It is loaded with Dimebucker pickups and Floyd Rose tremolo and has black hardware to set off the finish. The Slime Bumblebee part of the name refers to the green striped finish.

Kevin Deane Metallica Logo Guitar

Kevin Deane is a guitar enthusiast and builder from Ireland who enjoys experimenting with intricate designs, sometimes incorporating a band's logo. The Metallica guitar is based on the original logo that appears on the group's "Kill Em All" album. Kevin noticed that the shape was not very different from a Flying V. The wood used for the body is maple ply, which adds extra strength to the unusual shape and also provides a very dense in-structure with no voids. The guitar features a simple set-up: single humbucker, single volume control and hardtail bridge. The Flying V-like headstock complements the body style perfectly. (see picture below)

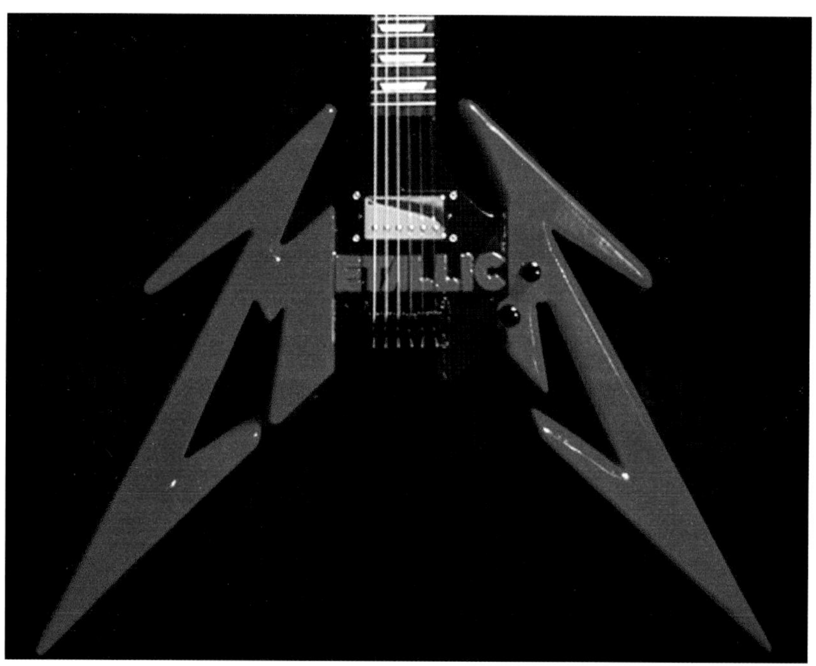

DeArmond Jet StarGuitar

The DeArmond Jet Star has a very peculiar shape with a Bo Diddley vibe, although it is actually the same design as the Guild Thunderbird that Muddy Waters used to play. Since DeArmond was taken over by Guild, this was probably a marketing tactic to release an old design under a new name - more recently the Guild brand was acquired by Fender and the DeArmond brand has now all but vanished. The layout of this guitar is pretty standard fare, with a pair of humbuckers and volume/tone for each. The sound is said to be similar to an SG but with a voice of its own.

Dega Morbidoni 2V

Dega Morbidoni was an accordion manufacturer in Italy's Castelfidaro who lent its name to guitars in the early 1960s beat boom. The first guitars bearing its name had glued-in necks and acrylic fingerboards and were virtually identical to early Bartolinis, but from 1963 bolt-on neck models appeared which made these instruments more distinctive. One of the most recognizable features of these was the Tele-like headstock. Finishes were usually highly glittery and the number of pickups ranged from one to four, depending on model.

DeGannaro Acoustic Bell

The Acoustic Bell is a hand-built acoustic from DeGennaro Guitars in Grand Rapids, Michigan. It has a full-bodied sound due, in part, to the unique soundhole configuration, which consists of a grouping of four holes laid out in the shape of a bell in the aged Sitka spruce top. Luthier Bill DeGennaro salvaged the spruce from a piano factory as well as some old ivory piano keys, which provided the material for the saddle. The back, sides and neck are all made of maple and the back features parquetry inlays. Fretboard, bridge and pickguard are of ebony, and the whole guitar is finished in nitrocellulose lacquer.

De Lacugo Guitars Excelsior

The De Lacugo Excelsior is a guitar guaranteed to turn heads. Finished in eye-catching glitter that would out-sparkle even the glitteriest of vintage Italian guitars and with a highly sculpted 3D body full of curves and contours plus a handle-like hole at the rear - this is not a guitar you could quickly forget. The headstock is also sculpted and drenched in glitter, whereas the fingerboard - which is one area where other guitars do sometimes feature some self-indulgent inlay work – is actually quite plain. Pickups are the usual two humbuckers and the guitar also features a locking tremolo and nut.

DeLaney Arlen Roth Signature Model

The name Arlen Roth should be familiar to a generation who grew up learning guitar from his "Hot Licks" instructional cassettes and videotapes. His signature guitar has been built by Mike Delaney of Delaney Guitars in Atlanta, Georgia, and should be immediately recognizable as a guitar based on the now legendary Telecaster. With a scale length of 25.5", maple neck, Grover tuners and Amalfitano TP pickups, what really makes the guitar stand out is that the alder body has been wrapped in hand-stitched aged-leather by master leathersmith, Tony Murga.

DePinto Belverdere Deluxe Bass

The Belverdere Deluxe Bass from DePinto is a retro-looking singlecut hollow-bodied instrument that certainly carries a lot of bling. The mahogany body may be finished in a sober black but is fitted with a large sparkling pickguard. There is also plenty of sparkle up at the headstock, while the maple neck itself is topped off with a 24-fret ebony fingerboard with star-shaped inlays. The pickups are shiny too, being chromed singlecoils. Those who like the general layout of the bass but can't look at it without wearing sunglasses might want to check out the less showy Belvedere Standard Bass instead, which is similar in design but has a more sober finish. (see picture below)

DePinto Galaxie 4

The Galaxie 4 is another glitter-encrusted guitar from DePinto of Philadelphia, PA, and appears to be a tribute to the weird and wonderful 1960s-era Italian guitars. It is possibly one of the few guitars in modern production sporting four singlecoil pickups. The pickup on/off switches on the upper horn call to mind the banks of pushbuttons that festooned the vintage guitars that this emulates. However, being built with quality materials (mahogany, maple and rosewood for the body, neck and fingerboard respectively) it plays a lot better than the old guitars. The Galaxie 4 is a favorite of surf band Los Straitjackets.

Desert Rose Double 10 Pedal Steel

To most "normal" guitarists, pedal steels are like something from outer space. They stand on legs while the player sits behind them; they typically have 10-strings - sometimes more - per neck; many have two necks usually tuned to C6 and E9; they are played with a steel bar in the left hand and fingerpicks in the right; and then there are all those pedals and levers! The Desert Rose Double 10 is such an example. It has 8 pedals and 5 knee levers, which are employed to effect various different pitch changes to the two 10-string necks. The trademark slurring sound heard in country music is created by using such pitch shifts during a song.

DeVillain Centerfold

Travel guitars come in many forms: some have full-scale lengths but have minimalist bodies and headless necks; others are diminutive guitars of shorter scale lengths, while others still break down into their component parts and are re-assembled at will. And then there is the DeVillain guitar, which is a normal-sized electric with the usual body and headstock and which doesn't need to be taken apart and put back together again. Its secret weapon is that it has a folding mechanism allowing the neck to be folded 180 degrees towards the body so that the guitar can fit into an easily manageable case.

DOBRO

Dewey Decibel's Flip-out Guitar

Dewey Decibel's Flip-out guitar is one of those instruments that makes you do a double-take when you first see it. Put quite simply, he's taken a Strat-type body and attached the neck to the wrong end. Despite the novelty nature of the instrument, the craftsmanship is of a high standard and the guitar is a beautiful player. Famous players include Nick Zinner of the Yeah Yeah Yeahs. A Bottom-out Bass is also available, and the guitar may also be the inspiration behind Gibson's Reverse Flying V.

Dobro M62 "Spanish Dancer"

Dobro's M62 "Spanish Dancer" guitar was available from 1935 to 1940 and is a nickel-plated brass-bodied resonator guitar similar to National's Style O series. Features particular to this model include the "fiddle edge" lips on the top and back edges of the body, the round window sound ports, and the sandblasted artwork to the body of the guitar which includes a scene portraying a female Spanish dancer on the back.

Dobro Hound Dog Squareneck

The Hound Dog Squareneck is a current production model based on Dobro's traditional resonator guitars. As its name implies, the guitar has a square neck meaning that it should be played upon the lap with a steel slide (sometimes called "Hawaiian-style"). The design is kept simple with no fancy binding or ornamentation. The hand-rubbed vintage brown body is made of maple ply and is fitted with a 10" spider resonator cone beneath the bridge, and with a fan-design cover plate. The guitar is suited to bluegrass and country music styles.

Dobro Model 27

The Dobro Model 27 dates back to the 1930s and is another of their wooden-bodied resonators. These guitars were built at the height of the Great Depression and were, for the most part, inexpensive builds. Early Model 27s were squarenecks constructed of non-descript hardwood laminate; the body was unbound and sometimes stained with a faux wood grain, had painted-on frets and silver-painted hardware. Later models, while still relatively inexpensive, were finished in very dark brown with binding and rosewood fingerboard and were made available in both square and roundneck versions.

Domino Californian Rebel

Despite its name, which in no doubt conjures up images of sun, sea and surf, and a music scene populated by the likes of The Beach Boys and The Doors, the 60s-era Domino Californian Rebel was actually a Japanese import. The guitar is unusually shaped, possibly inspired by the Vox Phantom, and is of semi-hollow construction with a German carve relief to the top, faux wooden pickguard, a basic vibrato with an integrated mute, and two singlecoil pickups, the one at the neck is angled in Mosrite fashion. The headstock is slotted and resembles that of a Spanish guitar.

Dommenget Acoustic Flying V

They said it couldn't be done, but Germany's Boris Dommenget built the world's first acoustic Flying V guitars for Rudolf Schenker of heavy metal band The Scorpions. Despite the unusual shape for an acoustic, these guitars are of a traditional build-quality and construction woods used include flamed maple and rosewood. Later models have included a 12-string Flying V acoustic, a doubleneck Flying V acoustic and an acoustic Explorer for Matthias Jabs, also of The Scorpions. In more recent years Rudolf Schenker has switched to playing Flying V acoustics built by Dean Guitars.

Doolin 20-string Harp Guitar

Doolin Guitars produce contemporary handcrafted guitars which are highly customizable to a customer's individual requirements. The 20-string harp guitar is a particularly exotic example. As well as the regular six-string neck it has an extended body arm on its bass side upon which are mounted six sub-bass strings, each of which has a lever allowing the player to quickly change keys. On the treble side of the body are a further eight strings with fine tuners at the bridge. It's an extremely beautiful instrument, although one that would baffle most players.

Doolin OM

The Doolin OM is an acoustic guitar from their standard range of instruments, which also includes jumbo, dreadnought, and classical guitars. As with all their instruments, the design features Doolin's own distinctive double-cutaway. Timbers used are Sitka spruce for the top, Indian rosewood for back and sides, mahogany for the neck, ebony for the fretboard and bridge, and binding of plain maple.

Dot On Shaft 2B1 Doubleneck

Most doubleneck guitars have two necks of differing kinds, for example 12-string and 6-string, or bass and 6-string. On the Dot On Shaft 2B1 model, however, both necks are 6-string. The guitar has two distinct personalities: the top half is based on a Telecaster while the bottom is all Les Paul. This is perfect for the guitarist who wants to have a Tele twang rhythm sound and then switch to a blistering solo all in the space of one song. Some would say you could achieve a similar result with modern effects units, but that would deny the chance to experiment with crazy guitars like this.

Doolin

Dramm Guitars The Botar

The Botar created by Thomas Dramm is a guitar specifically designed to be played with a bow, like a violin. To allow accurate bowing, the radiuses of the fingerboard and bridge are much more curved than on a regular guitar. The pickups also follow this curve, so as to capture an even sound across each of the strings. The body is chamfered on either side of the front to allow the bow access to the highest and lowest strings. Jimmy Page famously played electric guitar with a bow, but only a guitar with this design allows the player to bow individual notes. (see picture below)

Driskill Guitars Kurt Diablo's Guitar

Kurt Diablo had very specific requirements when ordering a guitar from Driskill Guitars. Kurt is quadriplegic so needed a guitar he could play using a stick held in his mouth. The neck is parallel along its length and has rails on either side. A claw rides on these, with a steel bar beneath it that does the fretting and a device to pick the strings: all of this is operated by the mouthstick. The guitar is covered in carbon fiber with an aluminum tribal inlay, and the tuners are upward facing so that they can be adjusted using the mouthstick.

Duesenberg D-Bass

Duesenberg guitars are designed by Dieter Goeldorf and assembled in Hannover, Germany. They produce high-class instruments with retro good looks and art deco-inspired features. The D-Bass is Duesenberg's first long-scale bass, and while the outline is reminiscent of Fender's Precision, its elegantly contoured body adds an element of luxury. A "hidden-bolt-on" neck joint effects the smooth transition from neck to body and the single toaster pickup employs a cunning "mid-shape" control to change its tonal character. The pickup can also switch between parallel and serial mode making for a large palette of sounds from a single-pickup bass.

Duesenberg Mike Campbell

The Duesenberg Mike Campbell signature was created to celebrate Campbell's career and 30-year anniversary of the band he plays for, Tom Petty and the Heartbreakers. It is an attractive hollow-bodied singlecut guitar, with elements of both the Les Paul and Gretsch guitars in its design, while the scale length is a Fender-like 25.5". The body has an arched spruce top on a maple back with a sustain center block. The 22-fret neck is American hardrock maple with a 12" radius Indian rosewood fingerboard. The guitar is fitted with Duesenberg pickups and their own take on the Bigsby vibrato and has a blue Hot Rod finish.

W.J. Dyer & Bro. Harp Guitar

Although each Dyer harp guitar carries a label claiming to be "manufactured by W.J. Dyer & Bro.", Dyer was merely the distributor. From 1899 to 1902 the guitars were built by Knutsen, and from 1902-1939 they were built on commission by brothers August and Carl Larson. The Larsons' harp guitar was based on the Knutsen design with a hollow body extension on the bass side holding between five and seven harp strings. The Larson brothers developed five different models for Dyer, the most celebrated of which was the Symphony #8 which featured a tree-of-life fingerboard inlay in mother of pearl and had six sub-bass strings.

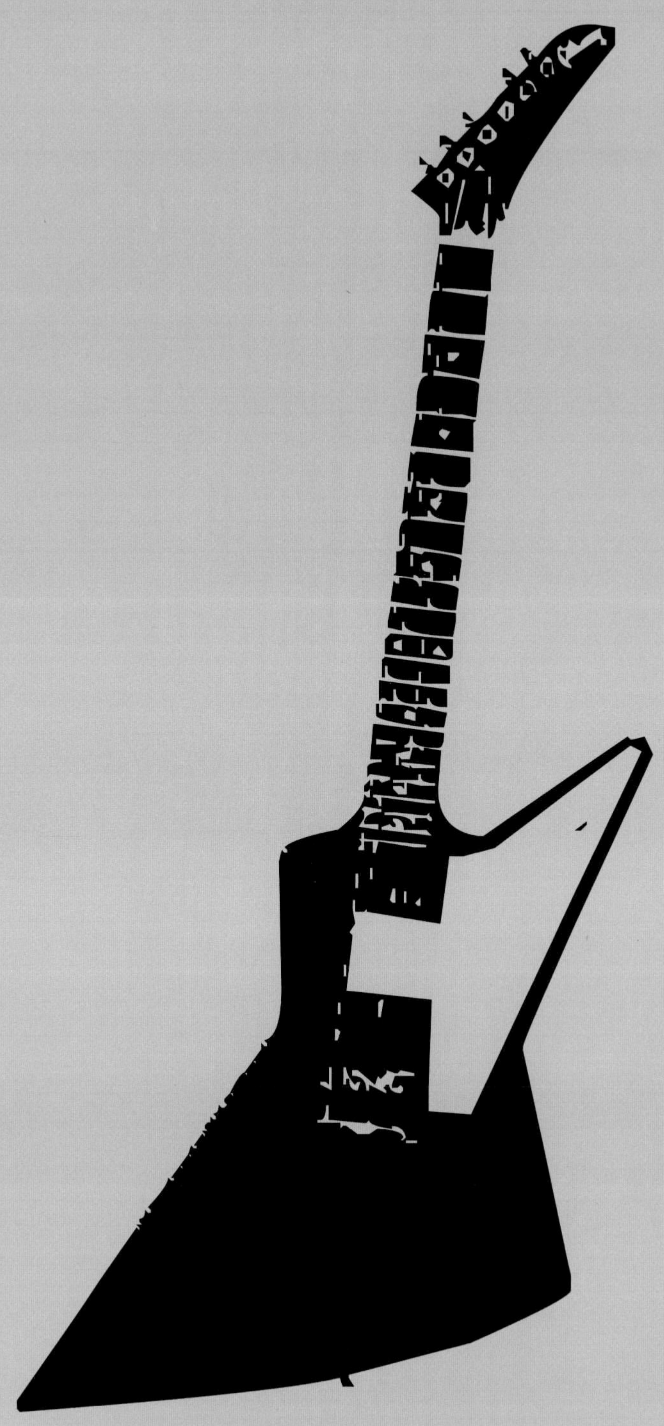

Earnest Instruments Flying TV Tenor Guitar

Tenor guitars first appeared in the 1920s. Featuring a shorter scale length than a regular guitar and only four strings, they were developed for players familiar with the tenor banjo. The Flying TV from Earnest Instruments brings the tenor guitar up-to-date and is an electric tenor version of the famous Flying V guitar. It features a mahogany bolt-on neck with rosewood fingerboard on a body of mahogany, alder or limba. The scale length, in keeping with its predecessors, is 23". Kent Armstrong mini-humbuckers, Grover tune-o-matic bridge and Gotoh tuners complete the collection.

Eastman Pagelli Series: PG1

Eastman is a Chinese manufacturer of acoustic - mainly archtop - guitars and mandolins. The Pagelli PG1 was designed in Switzerland by Claudio and Claudia Pagelli, and is a stylized archtop built from AAA spruce and maple. Its offset body features two modern f-holes, maple pickguard, bridge and tailpiece. Ebony is used for the fingerboard and headstock veneer. A floating Kent Armstrong pickup is mounted at the end of the fingerboard while the volume and tone controls are hidden discretely behind the pickguard. It is a very attractive guitar for the jazz musician who dares to be different.

Brian Eastwood Distortocaster

The Brian Eastwood Distortocaster looks the way a Fender Stratocaster would if it was been left out in the sun on a very hot day and melted. This guitar really has to be seen to be believed; if you view it edge-on, you can see that the body is bent in three dimensions. The pickups are crooked, the tremolo appears to be wonky, the neck distorts out-of-line at the higher frets and the headstock is skewed. It looks like a disaster but is reportedly an exceedingly good playing and sounding guitar. Motörhead's Phil Campbell occasionally pulls out a Distortocaster for encores. (see picture opposite)

Bender

Eccleshall Scimitar

Christopher J. Eccleshall of Devon, UK, is an authorized repairer of Martin, Gibson and Guild guitars, and also builds guitars and other fretted instruments under his own brand. His range of electric guitars includes those influenced by Gibson and Fender, and some completely original designs. One such design is the Scimitar, which is a 24.75" scale length guitar with a small tulip-shaped body, white binding and two humbuckers with individual volume and tone controls. The guitar can be customized from the standard configuration to suit the customer's requirements.

Egmond Typhoon

Egmond were a Dutch company producing guitars in the 1960s beat boom. Their guitars were almost as eccentric as those coming out of Italy during the same period. Influenced by the Fender Jazzmaster, the Typhoon appears to be a solid body but is actually of semi-hollow construction. The body is vinyl covered and has a pickguard and headstock facing of pearloid plastic (often referred to as "mother of toiletseat"). Other features include an approximation of the Jazzmaster tremolo, three pickups, volume, tone and seven-position rotary switch. Because of the cheap construction methods employed, examples in a playable condition are very rare.

Eko Model 700

If there were a classic guitar design to come out of 1960s Italy, the award would probably go to the Eko Model 700. Sometimes referred to as the Triple Cutaway because of the extra cutaway on the lower bout, the guitar was available in three and four pickup versions and a variety of finishes including vinyl covered and glitter-encrusted as were popular on European guitars of the era. As well as the usual volume and tone controls, the 700 had a bank of six switches set above the pickups. Famous players include Mark Knopfler who used the guitar on his "Shangri-La" album. (see picture below)

Eko Rokes

The Eko Rokes was a late 60s-era rocket-shaped guitar from one of Italy's finest guitar makers, and came with many different configurations: one or two pickups; with and without Bigsby vibrato; six-string, 12-string and bass; solid and semi-acoustic, etc. The guitar was originally designed for beat combo The Rokes, sometimes dubbed the Italian Beatles, who were a big hit in their native country in the mid to late 1960s. The Rokes guitar and bass were re-issued in more recent years by Eastwood guitars, who specialize in playable retro replicas. Players have included Julian Cope and Doggen Foster from Cope's band.

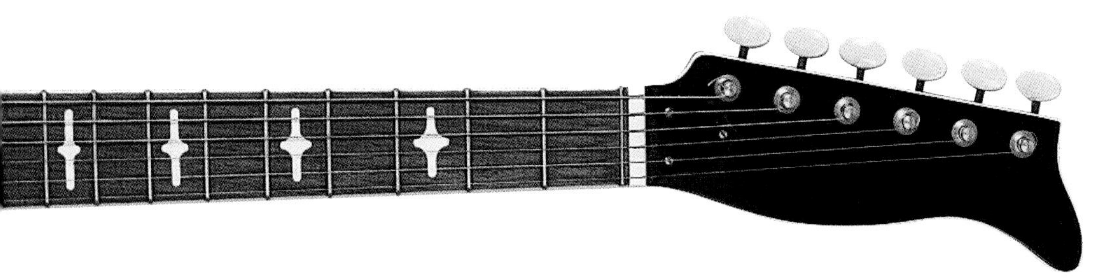

Emerald XB Bass

The XB-Bass is a very modern take on the acoustic bass guitar from Ireland's Emerald Guitar Company. Available in four and five-string versions, it is a sleek-looking bass sculpted from composite materials. The contoured body has an integral thumb rest above the strings and features an offset 3D soundport on the bass-side shoulder, which projects sound both forwards and up towards the player. Body and neck are one-piece carbon graphite, the fingerboard is carbon fiber and electronics are B-Band 4 band EG and under saddle transducers.

Emerald The Alien

The Alien is truly a one-off from the custom shop of Ireland's Emerald Guitar Company, and reportedly took 400 hours to build. If guitar designing were an extreme sport then this beastie would take the prize. Finished in silver and looking like something from H.R. Giger's nightmares, the Alien is one seriously weird but highly intriguing piece of engineering. Part guitar and part sculpture, the most unusual feature is the limb that snakes out from the body's bass side, arches over the top of the fingerboard and continues up to the head where it merges into the headstock. File under "scary". (see detail of the alien above and another Emerald right)

Epiphone 1910 Harp Guitar

The 1910 Harp Guitar has been preserved for prosperity in Epiphone's own museum of vintage guitars. It has a large black cutaway body with heart-shaped soundhole, one regular six-string neck and a secondary neck (or perhaps "arm" would be a better word) upon which six sub-bass strings are strung. Two six-in-a-line headstocks face one another like mirror images; the head of the regular neck has three extra holes drilled into it, as if at some point in its life the guitar had even more strings. Inside the guitar is the original "House of Stathopoulo" label, referring to the founders of the company that was to be re-named Epiphone.

Epiphone Airscreamer

The Epiphone Airscreamer is a puzzling piece of design: why make a guitar that resembles an Airstream trailer? The guitar has a 24.75" scale length, a pair of EMG HZ humbuckers positioned to look like windows, a single volume control disguised as the hub cap on the trailer's wheel, and a body that looks like a caravan! This is a hard one to get your head around. Who is it meant to appeal to? It's like an uncool version of Bo Diddley's square guitar, but it is definitely unique.

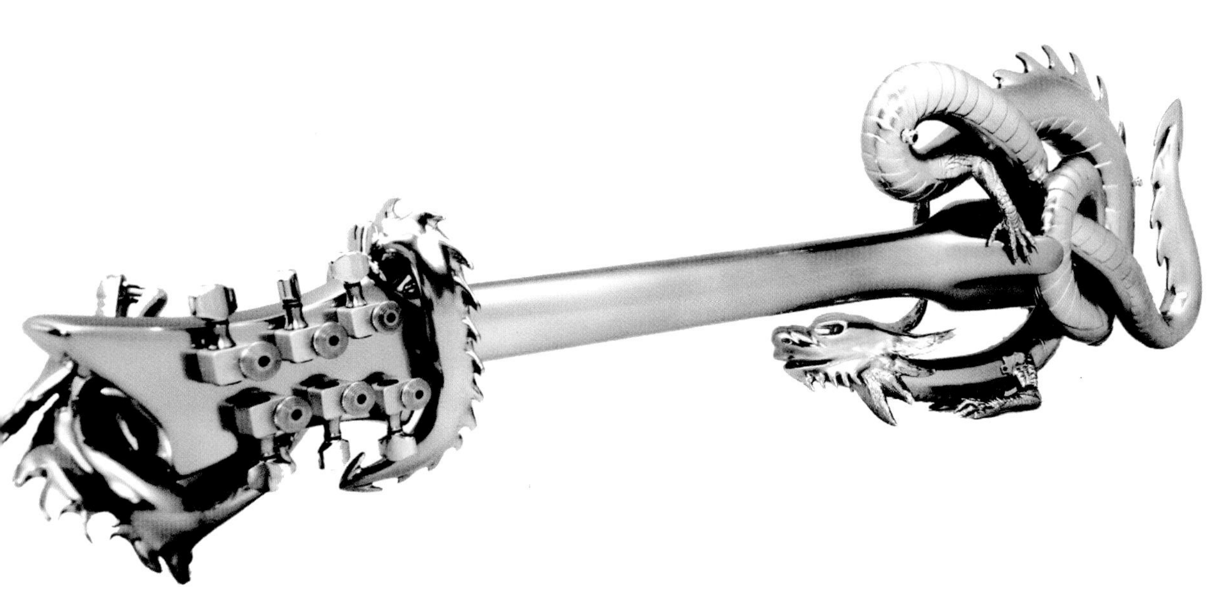

Epiphone Blackstone Tenor Guitar

The Epiphone Blackstone first appeared in 1931 and stayed in production for 20 years. Its bound body was constructed with maple back and sides and a carved spruce top bearing a pair of f-holes. It also had a raised pickguard, adjustable bridge and trapeze tailpiece. The neck had a twenty-fret rosewood fingerboard with pearl dot inlays and joined the body at the 14th fret. The four-stringed tenor guitar version of the same model entered production in 1937 and lasted until 1949. This model featured parallelogram fingerboard inlays and a sunburst finish.

Epiphone Jack Casady Bass

When Epiphone engineers worked in close collaboration with Jack Casady, the bassist with Jefferson Airplane and Hot Tuna, the result was this semi-hollow archtop signature series bass. The body design is modeled closely on the little-known Les Paul Signature semi-hollow guitar. This is a big-bodied 34" scale instrument with a three-point bridge and a single low-impedance humbucker - the JCB-1 - developed especially for this bass. The sound is said to be articulate, warm and deep. (see picture below)

Epiphone Recording 4

The Epiphone Recordng 4, circa 1930, is a luxurious acoustic guitar with an elongated asymmetrical body-shape featuring a sloping cutaway on the treble side. The back is arched and made of birds' eye maple, the sides are maple and the top is of hand-carved spruce. The front of the guitar is fitted with a raised celluloid pickguard. It has a maple neck and a highly decorated plastic veneered headstock that resembles that of a banjo, complete with non-geared tuners with ivory buttons. The fingerboard is rosewood with decorative celluloid inlays.

Epiphone Scroll 550

The 550 was the top-of-the-line model in the Scroll series that saw production from 1976 to 1979. It is a Japanese-made double cutaway Les Paul-style guitar with a distinctive scrolled upper horn. The body and neck are both solid maple, and the fingerboard is ebony with block inlays. Electrics are a pair of humbuckers with volume, tone, three-way switch and coil cut. There were two finishes available, natural or ebony, both being accompanied with gold hardware. Sound-wise, the tone has been compared to a Les Paul, and being made of solid maple it is a guitar of similar weight. (see picture above)

Epiphone Double Scroll Bass

The Epiphone Double Scroll Bass was the bass companion to the Scroll guitar series of the late 1970s and was also made in Japan. It is of similar construction to the Scroll guitar with the same German carve to the top, but has a couple of individual features of its own, the most obvious being that both horns are scroll-shaped. The rounded shape of the top end of the fingerboard where it meets the body also differs from the Scroll, together with the large pickguard carrying the pickups and electrics which is not present on the guitar model.

Epiphone Wildkat

Epiphone, a subsidiary of Gibson, clearly borrowed elements of the legendary Les Paul when designing this guitar, but extended the lines to make this archtop a bit curvier than its predecessor. The bridge is set up with a Bigsby-style vibrato bar for effortless play and a truly tremendous sound. Heavier strings are necessary to make the most of the mahogany body and pickups, and get it singing like a real wildcat. (see picture below)

Epiphone Wilshire

The Epiphone Wilshire was originally released in 1960, just three years after Gibson purchased the company, and was built in Kalamazoo, Michigan. With a lightweight double cutaway body allowing access to each of the 22 frets, it was a competitor to Fender's Stratocaster. The body is made from solid mahogany and features electrics reminiscent of its Gibson cousin, the Les Paul Junior. It has two P90 pickups with a volume and tone for each and a 3-way selector, and also had an intonable bridge - an advantage over the simpler junior. Epiphone reissued the guitar in 2009 and the first batch of 100 sold out immediately.

Erlewine Chiquita

In the opening scenes of the movie "Back To The Future" we see Marty McFly (Michael J. Fox) plug a little guitar into an amp hooked up to an unfeasibly large speaker and unleash chaos as he strikes a chord. That guitar - if you ever wondered - is a Erlewine Chiquita, the original travel guitar designed by Mark Erlewine and ZZ Top's Billy Gibbons. Made of solid Honduras mahogany with a bound body and head, 19" scale, rosewood fingerboard, humbucker and single volume, and weighing only 4.5lbs, this guitar packs a lot of punch into a small package.

Ernie Ball Earthwood Acoustic Bass

Made between 1975 and 1985, the Earthwood is a behemoth of a bass. Unlike some acoustic basses, which are merely bass versions of acoustic guitar models, the Earthwood was designed specifically as an acoustic bass. The body (walnut with a spruce top) is absolutely huge and nearly 7" deep. It has a 34" scale, but may not appeal to players who like to play at the top of the neck since the maple neck and fingerboard has only 16 frets, and the neck joins the body at the 12th. The sound can be described as phenomenal and very loud. Players include Brian Ritchie of the Violent Femmes. (see picture opposite)

ESP GazettE A-I

Take one look at ESP's GazettE A-I model and you know it's designed for metal. The alder body is a jagged, heavily carved singlecut shape and completely finished in black. The hard maple neck has a 24-fret ebony fingerboard continuing the color scheme. Unusually, it has four pickups with both Lace Sensor and Seymour Duncans at the neck and bridge positions. Despite this the controls are kept simple with just a single volume and two switches. A Floyd Rose tremolo and Gotoh tuners complete the hardware.

ESP Devil Girl

ESP's Devil Girl guitar is one that some will love while others will point and laugh. The blood red body appears to be heavily carved - although it is actually molded from a dense "secret recipe" plastic resin - and portrays the eponymous Devil Girl in a reclining position with her bat-like wings spread out behind her. The resulting shape is not too far away from the Explorer body style, but unfortunately has a negative effect on playability, as only 15 of the 22 frets are easily accessible. Electrics are a lone EMG HZ humbucker and a volume control.

ESP Jeune Fille X Bronze

ESP's Jeune Fille X is the signature model for Mana, guitarist with Japanese theatrical rock band Moi dix Mois. The body is formed of alder with a heavily carved maple top and is shaped somewhat like a violin with two heavily extended scrolled horns. The headstock on the 3-ply maple neck is also a scroll shape with a two-over-four tuner layout. Fingerboard inlays spell out "jeune fille" (young girl). Electrics are kept simple with a single EMG 81 humbucker and volume control, and the tremolo is by Kahler.

ESP LTD Standard PB Series

The ESP LTD Standard PB series guitars are much less radical in design than many of their diabolically designed stable mates, most of which are intended primarily as shred machines. The versatile Seymour Duncan P-Rail pickups are powerful but, at the same time, able to transmit nuances of the guitar's own acoustic properties unlike certain other pickups which you could probably mount on a shovel and still get the same sound. Body and neck are made of mahogany with a 22-fret rosewood fingerboard. These classy guitars demonstrate perfectly that ESP is not a one-trick pony.

Espana VL-107 Winged Guitar

The Landola company in Finland, whose most notable and intriguing models are "winged" guitars, produced Espana classical guitars. Some have a single wing on the bass side similar to the extended body bout reaching towards the headstock seen on harp guitars, while others such as the SL-107 model have a wing on either side. Unlike most harp guitars, there are no additional strings. One theory is that the wings are supposed to resemble the raised arms of a Spanish flamenco dancer. However, it is more likely that they serve to enrich the tone and sound projection, as these guitars reportedly exhibit an incredible resonance and deep bass tone. (see picture opposite)

Etavonni

Etavonni may sound like another Italian brand, but it's actually "innovate" spelled backwards and the company is based in Michigan. The innovation in these guitars is in their use of cutting edge materials designed to deliver a rich and consistent tone. Specifically, Etavonni guitars feature a 25" scale carbon fiber neck with 22-fret ebony fingerboard, mounted onto a body frame of machined aircraft grade anodized aluminum finished with carbon fiber panels in the front and back. Other features include Planet Waves locking tuners, Hipshot hardtail bridge, and Seymour Duncan pickups. A Wilkinson Gotoh tremolo is optional.

Espana
Espana

Faith FM Mercury Parlour

Faith acoustic guitars are manufactured in the Far East, but designed by British luthier Patrick James Eggle (not to be confused with the other Patrick Eggle). The FM Mercury is a parlor-sized acoustic, elegant in its simplicity. Built from Indonesian mahogany with a solid Engelmann spruce top, the Mercury has a natural sweet tone. The neck - with a Macassar ebony fingerboard - joins the body at the 12th fret, which is said to improve the resonance in small-bodied acoustics such as this. The guitar is finished with polyurethane lacquer on the top and satin finish on back and sides.

Fender Bass VI

Released in 1961, the Fender Bass VI was an oddity. Was it a bass or was it a guitar? Its six strings were tuned like a guitar but an octave lower like a bass, and it had a 30" scale. It was possibly the first bass to have a tremolo. Electrics were three single-coil pickups with individual on/off switches and, later, a fourth switch for bass cut. String spacing was too cramped for many bass players, but made it more suitable for guitarists. Some used heavy gauge guitar strings and a baritone tuning. Famous players include Jack Bruce, Noel Redding from The Jimi Hendrix Experience, and Robert Smith of The Cure.

Fender Coronado

Best known for its solid-bodied electric guitars, Fender has also dabbled with hollow-bodied electrics such as the Coronado, available from 1966 to 1972. It was designed by Roger Rossmeisl, who had also designed several Rickenbacker guitars. The top and back of the body were made of laminated beech wood, with the top being gently arched. The maple neck was bolt-on, as on other Fenders, and carried the familiar but slightly modified Fender 6-in-a-line headstock. Pickups were by DeArmond and the guitar also had an un-Fender-like tune-o-matic bridge and suspended tailpiece. A 12-string and bass were also available.

Fender Electric XII

The Electric XII was designed by Leo Fender himself and was in production from 1965-1969. It was conceived as a 12-string right from the start and was not just a variant of an existing model. The body was of alder and had a bolt-on maple neck with a "hockey-stick" headstock designed to accommodate all 12 tuners. Two split single coil pickups allowed for series and parallel options when selecting both at once. Notable players include Pete Townshend of The Who and Roy Wood of The Move and Wizzard, while Jimmy Page used an Electric XII when recording "Stairway To Heaven".

Fender Jaguar

The Jaguar, launched as Fender's top-of-the-line model in 1962, was essentially a shorter, 24" scale version of the Jazzmaster. It had similar circuitry to that used by the Bass VI including the "strangle" switch, which engaged a high-pass filter to deliver a treble-enhanced tone. It had two re-designed single coil pickups that were less prone to interference than those of the Strat and Tele. The guitar was an instant favorite on the surf music scene, and many years later caught the imagination of the indie rock crowd. Notable players include Sonic Youth, Brian Molko of Placebo, and John Frusciante of the Red Hot Chili Peppers. (see picture below)

Fender Jazz Bass

As Fender's second bass guitar model, the Jazz Bass was an evolution of the Precision Bass with an offset waist contour body. It was so named because it was thought that its narrower neck would appeal to jazz musicians. Two single coil pickups, with two pole pieces per string, gave it a brighter tone with a stronger midrange than its predecessor. Players of note include session man Herbie Flowers, Led Zeppelin's John Paul Jones, and Jaco Pastorius of Weather Report who removed the frets from his "Bass of Doom" and popularized the fretless bass.

Fender Jazzmaster

Debuting in 1958, the Jazzmaster was the first of Fender's guitars to feature a body with an offset waist contour. It was also their first with a maple neck with separate rosewood fingerboard. Fender intended that this guitar would replace the Telecaster, and - as might be guessed from its name - they initially tried marketing the guitar to jazz players. However, it was not a hit in these circles. Features include a 25" scale, lead and rhythm circuit switching, and a long-armed floating tremolo with a lock to stop the guitar going out of tune in the event of string breakage. (see picture on opposite page)

"My vocation is more in composition really than anything else - building up harmonies using the guitar, orchestrating the guitar like an army, a guitar army."
- Jimmy Page

Fender Katana

The Katana is possibly the most un-Fender-like guitar ever produced by that company. Dating from 1985, the Katana had a pointed triangular body shape, which was aimed at the same sector of the market as V-derived, sharkfin-style guitars such as the Jacksons Randy Rhoads. It had further non-Fender features such as a 24.75" scale, a glued-in neck, and pointed headstock with an angular Fender logo. Electrics comprised two humbuckers, volume, tone and 3-way switch, all mounted from the rear. A single-pickup, bolt-on neck Squier version was also available. Both were made in Japan and were available for only one year before being discontinued.

Fender Mustang

Beloved by indie musicians today, the short-scale Mustang guitar was conceived as a student model in 1964. Its styling was similar to earlier budget Fenders, the Duo-Sonic and Musicmaster, but with an offset waist. Two scale lengths were offered: 21-fret 22.5" and 22-fret 24", with the latter achieving greater popularity. It was the first Fender student guitar equipped with a tremolo - the Fender Dynamic Vibrato - which is almost legendary among aficionados and a large part of what made the Mustang so popular on the indie rock scene. Players have included: Adrian Belew of King Crimson, David Byrne of the Talking Heads) and Nirvana's Kurt Cobain. (see picture below)

Fender Precision Bass

One of Leo Fender's most famous designs, the Precision Bass first hit the marketplace in 1951 and was the first mass-produced electric bass. It was called "Precision" because it was fretted, allowing accurate playing. Earlier examples were slab-bodied and more in keeping with its stable mate, the Telecaster. Models from 1953 had contoured edges, but it wasn't until 1957 that the Precision Bass that we know today was born, having been redesigned to complement the then-new Stratocaster. The single coil pickup of the original was replaced with a split-coil pickup, which functioned as a humbucker, and more Strat-like contouring, pickguard and larger headstock were added.

Fender Princeton Lap Steel

The Fender Princeton Lap Steel was made from 1946 to 1948. It is quite a primitive instrument made from a single piece of ash and featuring art-deco styling, metal fingerboard with Roman numeral markers and a metal plate at the base of the body carry the rectangular string-through pickup, bridge and single volume control. A metal plate on the headstock features an engraved lightning bolt logo bearing the legend "Fender Electric Instrument Co, Fullerton, California".

Fender Stratocaster

The Strat was developed in 1954 but only achieved popularity after 1957 when Buddy Holly appeared with his version on the Ed Sullivan Show. Since then, it has been a favorite of many musicians including Jimi Hendrix, who had his 1969 Woodstock Strat auctioned off for a record $270,000 in 1990. A fast action maple neck and comfort contoured Alder body mean this guitar fits like a glove and has achieved classic status.

Fender Stringmaster Console Guitar

The Fender Stringmaster is a console guitar, which is played in a similar fashion to a lap steel. However, possessing two or more necks, its size is impractical for playing upon the lap and so it stands on legs allowing the player to sit behind it. It resembles a pedal steel but without the pedals and levers. Enabling the player to have several different tunings, the Stringmaster was available in two, three and four-neck models, each neck having eight strings. They were produced from 1953 right up until 1980, except the four-neck which was discontinued in 1968. A single-neck version with six or eight strings was known as the Fender Deluxe.

Fender Telecaster

Another from the family of Fender classics, the Tele was the first guitar of its kind to be produced on a substantial scale. Known for its bright, cutting tone, this guitar achieved notoriety swinging from the shoulders of Elvis, George Harrison and Keith Richards. The design is relatively simple – carved into a slab instead of curving like its later sibling, the Stratocaster, but that's part of the Tele's charm. Simplicity and durability have made this into a timeless classic.

"I remember one time I was running from one side of the stage to the other, and I suddenly noticed Axl was running from the opposite direction and that I wasn`t going to be able to get out of his way. Immediately went into a tuck and roll, and he jumped over the top of me. And I didn`t miss a note! It was cool." - Slash

Fernandes Nomad

The Nomad is a travel or practice guitar with a full-scale length, a kidney bean-shaped body with cutaway to the treble side letting it sit comfortably upon the knee, and a droopy-looking headstock. As well as a humbucking pickup and hardtail bridge it has a built-in amp and 4" speaker powered by a 9-volt battery. Controls are a single volume/on-off knob and an overdrive switch. Deluxe models feature built-in digital effects, and both Standard and Deluxe are available in a range of graphic finishes such as hot rod flame, USA flag and UK flag.

Fernandes Ravelle

The Ravelle is Fernandes' own re-interpretation of the Les Paul guitar. The shape is obviously derived from the LP, but with a few design twists. The Deluxe and Elite models each have a mahogany body with a Canadian maple carved top, while the more basic X model has the same design built from alder. All models have two humbuckers, but the Elite alone features a Fernandes Sustainer unit in the neck position, which energizes the guitar strings in a similar fashion to the handheld EBow and allows for infinite sustain. Unlike the EBow, the Sustainer affects all the strings at once rather than just a single string.

Fernandes UJL-2000

The Um Jammer Lammy guitar from Fernandes in Japan looks like a toy guitar or a guitar from a cartoon. Actually, that's not so far from the truth; its design is based on a guitar from a Playstation game. In turn, the guitar in the game was based on a Les Paul, so what we have here is a real guitar based on a fictional guitar based on a real guitar. Confused? The guitar has a short scale, and - surprisingly for what is in essence a novelty guitar - three P90 pickups.

FERNANDES
F.E.R. SUSTAINER

Fernandes Vertigo

The Vertigo is one of Fernandes' trademark designs. Its asymmetrical shape makes it look like a hard-rocking guitar. With a short 22" scale, the Deluxe and Elite models each feature a mahogany body, slim tapered set neck with 22-fret rosewood fingerboard featuring spilt trapezoid inlays. The Deluxe has tune-o-matic bridge and stop tailpiece and is fitted with a pair of EMGs, while the Elite has a Floyd Rose licensed tremolo, Fernandes Sustainer and EMG 81 pickups. The basic X model has a bolt-on neck, alder body and two humbuckers. (see another of the Fernandes creations opposite)

Ferrington KFS-2 Electro-acoustic

Danny Ferrington gained a reputation for his highly skilled luthiery, having built guitars for celebrities. His designs were the first to take an electro-acoustic guitar and give it the feel and the aesthetics of an electric. Teaming up with Kramer guitars in the mid 1980s several of his designs went into production in Korea. The KFS-2 is a Strat-shaped thin-bodied electro-acoustic with a rounded/triangular soundhole. The bolt-on maple neck has a pointed headstock and rosewood fingerboard with dot inlays. A passive piezo pickup is mounted in the bridge, while volume and tone controls are on the body's rim near the upper horn.

D. Fialho Drone Harp Guitar

The Drone Harp guitar is carved out of a single piece of Brazilian mahogany. The bottom neck is a six-string fretless guitar, the output from which is fed into a sealed acoustic chamber within the upper "neck" via a pair of 3" speakers. This causes the 12 drone strings of the harp section to resonate. Each neck has its own output jack so that signals can be sent to separate amps or mixer channels. The guitar also has the facility to bypass the lower fretless neck and plug an external sound source into the drone chamber.

FERNANDES

First Act Garagemaster

First Act builds guitars ranging from budget conscious to custom. In a 2006 campaign with Volkswagon of America Inc, those buying or renting certain VW cars would receive a free Garagemaster guitar. The guitar, with a shape borrowed from Brian May's Red Special, has a built-in pre-amp meaning it can be plugged directly into the VW's auxiliary jack, so the car itself acts as a mobile amp. Each guitar is finished in one of four VW-complimentary colours and has the vehicle identification number of the car it was supplied with engraved on the back of the headstock.

First Act Sheena

First Act's Sheena is an attractive single cutaway guitar which is designed to deliver a rich, jangly tone from its single P90-like Alnico V vintage-style pickup. With a body built from poplar and a maple bolt-on neck, this guitar has a Telecaster vibe. A sleeker twin pickup version shows us what a Tele might have looked like if it had been built by Gretsch. With a set neck and alder body with binding, this model is courtesy of First Act's Limited Edition series. (pictured right, Nick Zinner plays the Delia on the opposite page)

"With a guitar I would be able to express the things I felt in sounds."
- William Christopher Handy

Charles Fox Ergo

The Ergo is a stunning guitar built by Charles Fox. It is a luxurious high-performance instrument and features such innovations as a wedge-shaped body; elevated fingerboard, which positions strings at a steeper angle to the bridge; adjustable soundport in the top rim of the guitar; and a patented ultra-low mass soundboard - a sandwich of high-tech honeycomb material between two thin skins of tone wood, which means less weight to dampen harmonics. All of which adds up to make a guitar with an exceptional sound, rich in harmonic content with a broad range.

Frame Works Classical Guitar

The Frame Works Classical Guitar was developed for those requiring a classical or nylon-strung guitar in amplified situations where ordinarily they would rely on microphone set-ups. The guitar is formed from a hand-shaped mahogany neck-through body making up the central core of the guitar. A headless design means tuners are positioned behind the bridge making for a more compact instrument. Two foam-covered resonance tubes are attached to the center section to form the wings of the guitar in an approximation of the traditional classical guitar shape. Individual string sensors in the bridge provide string-to-string balance and optional MIDI access. A single 9V battery feeds the onboard active electronics. (see picture below)

Framus Star Bass

The Star Bass debuted at the Frankfurt music show in 1956. A short-scale hollow-bodied instrument of single cutaway design, the creators had hoped it would appeal to both guitar players and bassists tired of the logistics involved in carrying around a double bass. The bass had two pickups mounted adjacent to a pickguard carrying the volume and tone controls. The 1960s saw a larger bodied Star Bass, and this was the model made famous by Bill Wyman of the Rolling Stones. This model became known unofficially as the Stone Bass.

Framus Strato Deluxe

The Strato Deluxe clearly borrows its unusual waist design from the Fender Jaguar and Jazzmaster. Built from 1965 to the end of the 60s, the guitar is a solid body of sandwich construction. Its front is covered with a large chrome pickguard carrying a number of switches and knobs including those of a built-in pre-amp. Some similar guitars were said to have a built-in half-mechanical organ effect. Three singlecoil pickups are slanted at three different angles and a tremolo sits behind a very basic-looking bridge. The headstock shape varies on different examples from a Fender-clone to Framus' very own "flipper" design. (see a Framus custom creation below)

Esprit III
Ventura 60/60

Scott French Singlecut Bass

Scott French is a luthier based in Auburn, California, who handcrafts quality guitars and basses of his own design. The SF4 and SF5 singlecut basses are amalgamations of earlier designs. He has literally taken the treble side from one instrument and the bass side from another. The basses are of through-neck construction, with the shaped back of the neck continuing into the body to the depth of the cutaway. As each instrument is custom-built, the finer details vary from one instrument to the next. Timbers and hardware are chosen according to the tastes of the individual customer.

Fret King Green Label Esprit III

Fret King Guitars, designed by Trev Wilkinson, have two ranges - the UK hand-built Green Label series, and the more economical Blue Label produced in Korea. The Green Label Esprit III is a gorgeous guitar that seems to blend several classic designs. There is a definite nod to the Gibson Firebird in the raised center section of the body and in the reverse headstock, while the gentle curves of the cutaways are reminiscent of the Fender Jazzmaster. The Esprit III is built from korina, with a 25" scale, set neck and 12" radius rosewood fingerboard. Pickups are three P90s, the middle being reverse-wound, reverse-polarity for hum cancelling in positions 2 and 4. (see pictures of the red and gold models opposite)

"An uncle of mine emigrated to Canada and couldn't take his guitar with him. When I found it in the attic, I'd found a friend for life." - Sting

Fret Song FS-1

The FS-1 is a headless guitar of advanced design built from a choice of exotic timbers, featuring a chambered body with a solid center core. The body is highly comfort contoured at the rear and around the neck/body join area allowing completely clear access to all 24 frets. The top of the guitar has a mild arch from the center downward in all directions with recessed control knobs and pickup frames for a flush surface. Finishing touches include matching exotic timber used for the rear electronics cover and a signature inlayed ebony pickguard.

Froggy Bottom P-12

Froggy Bottom Guitars of Chelsea, Vermont, specialize in building individually handcrafted steel string flat top guitars. Necks are made from mahogany, but there is a choice of exotic tonewoods available for the tops, backs and sides, all of which are air-dried. The P-12 model is a parlor-sized guitar, with - as its model designation suggests - 12 frets clear of the body. Sound-wise it has a wide dynamic range, exhibiting sparkling highs and, despite its size, a dramatic bass response. (see picture below and opposite)

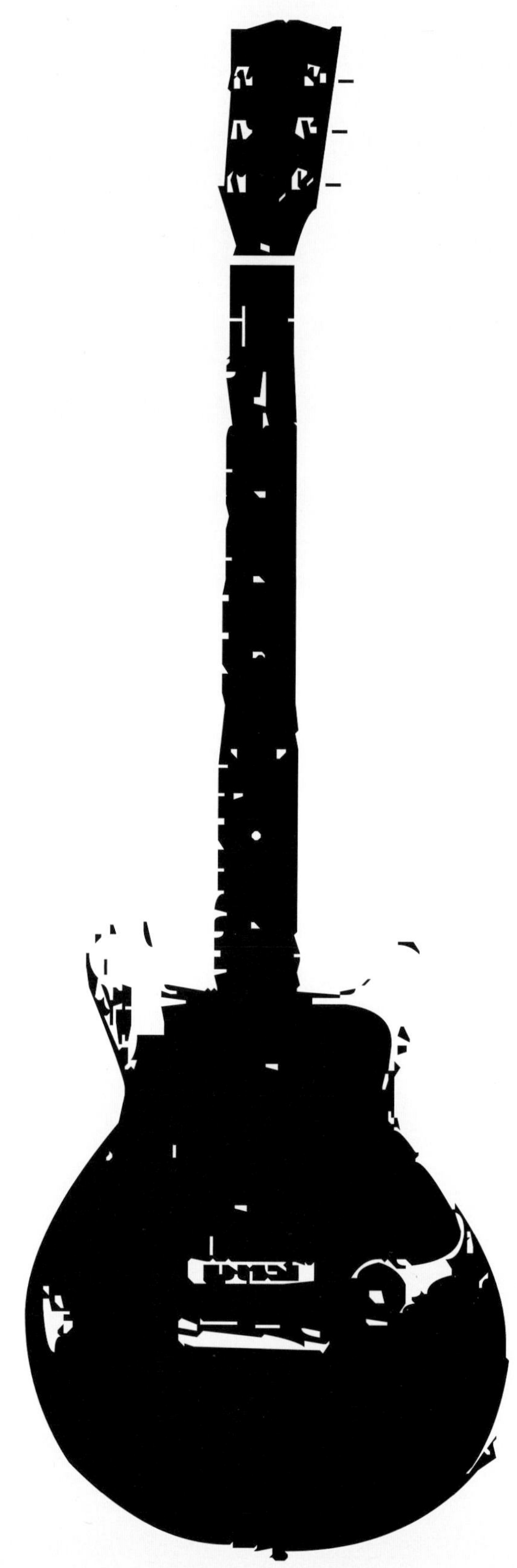

G&L SC-2

G&L was founded by Leo Fender along with George Fullerton and Dale Hyatt in 1979, with the SC-2 being one of their earliest production guitars. It was a no-nonsense, small-bodied guitar, aimed primarily at the same end of the market as Fender's Mustang and similar models. Body, neck and fingerboard are all made of maple, and the guitar has two Magnetic Field Design singlecoils producing a sound quite similar to that of a Telecaster. A tremolo-equipped version was also available. The guitar was popular with inveterate tinkerers as a basic instrument for performing upgrades. Notable users include Bob Mothersbaugh from Devo.

G&L ASAT

The ASAT is G&L's version of the Telecaster guitar, designed by Leo Fender to be an improvement on the original. The name of the guitar was Leo's little joke, referring to the guitars he'd spent a large portion of his life making and is an acronym for "Another Strat, Another Tele". Just like Fender's Tele, the ASAT has spawned a whole host of variants including semi-hollow models with f-holes, Bluesboy models with a humbucker in the neck position, and the Z-3 triple split-pickup models, among others.

G&L ASAT Bass Semi Hollow

Fender's Telecaster Bass was not very Tele-like with its double-cutaway design, and was really a renamed reissue of the original Precision Bass. However, G&L's ASAT Bass is recognizably Tele-like in design. The Semi-Hollow is a thinline version having a swamp ash body with two voice chambers. The f-hole is optional. The 21-fret neck is hard rock maple with a choice of rosewood or maple fingerboard. Pickups are two G&L Magnetic Field humbuckers, resembling those on Musicman basses. With features such as Tri-Tone active/passive electronics, series/parallel switch, and EQ boost, this bass has access to a wide palette of tones. (see picture below)

G&L Comanche

The Comanche is a high quality Strat-type guitar with three G&L Magnetic Field Design Z-coil split pickups. The Z-coils are very effective noise cancelling pickups and are very powerful, allowing for a wide range of tone options, but can be a little "sterile" for some tastes. It is a beautifully made instrument with alder or swamp ash body and a hard rock maple neck with rosewood or maple fingerboard.

Galanti Grand Prix Special

Galanti is another Italian accordion manufacturer that made the switch to guitars in the 1960s. The Grand Prix guitar is a mahogany-bodied, vaguely Strat-shaped guitar with three singlecoil pickups on a Z-shaped pickguard, and with the inevitable push buttons that the accordion manufacturers were so fond of. Unusually for 1960s Italian guitars, the finishes on these Galanti guitars are quite sober, mostly featuring dark sunbursts. The design of this guitar - if not the finish - may have been the inspiration behind DePinto's retro Galaxie 4 model. (see picture right)

Giannini Craviola 12-string

Giannini Craviola acoustic guitars are immediately recognizable with their half-lute/half-guitar body shape. Thankfully the guitar half is the one you rest upon your knee when seated! These guitars were made in Brazil and early models from the 1970s and 80s used laminated wood throughout. These guitars have a unique sound and quite a cult following. However, they have a reputation - especially in the cases of the top 12-string models - of suffering over time from warping tops and lifting bridges. It is possible that the stresses of a 12-string are too much for the laminated construction. A newer version of the Craviola 12-string is constructed from solid woods, and should not suffer from the same problems.

Champion

Gibson

Gibson BR-9 Lap Steel

The BR-9 was available from 1947 to 1959 and was Gibson's biggest selling lap steel from that period. It was also the least expensive. It has a graduated art deco-styled body finished in beige with a brownish-red combined pickup cover and control plate concealing the P90 pickup and bridge, upon which are two radio knobs for volume and tone. A similarly colored fingerboard has numbered open block position markers. The headstock is the same shape as that seen on Les Paul and SG electric guitars and carries 3-on-a-plate Kluson Deluxe tuners and a silkscreened Gibson logo.

Gibson Chet Atkins Studio CEC

Gibson's Chet Atkins series of "solidbody acoustics" was originally launched in 1981, giving the acoustic guitarist an instrument that could be played at volume without feedback. In 2003, Gibson's acoustic division in Montana unveiled the nylon-strung Chet Atkins Studio CEC, which is hollowbody to increase acoustic volume and a classical guitar nut width of 2 inches. Braces and tone bars beneath the top are carefully positioned to emulate the tone of Spanish builds such as Ramirez. The soundhole is positioned on the bass side of the fingerboard and a second oval soundhole in the upper back enhances the player's acoustic experience.

Gibson 1959 EB-0 Bass (LP Junior shape)

Gibson's 30.5" short scale EB-0 bass is a model familiar to many as the "SG-shaped bass". However, the first batch of EB-0s from 1959 to 1961 had a body design based on the double-cutaway Les Paul Junior and is arguably a much more attractive instrument. It is believed that around 500 such examples were built, and nowadays these are much sought after on the vintage market. The bass has a mahogany body and neck with a single large humbucker mounted near the neck, giving the EB-0 a thumpy sound, and the headstock is fitted with banjo-style tuners.

Gibson EDS-1275 doubleneck

The Gibson EDS-1275 is one of the most iconic guitars in rock. Over the years many players have risked back pain by strapping on this doublenecked leviathan, but it is most commonly associated with Led Zeppelin's Jimmy Page. Gibson's first doublenecks were produced in 1958 and were hollow-bodies based on the jazzy ES-175. The better known solid body double-SG design appeared in 1962. The body is solid mahogany with two set-in maple necks (12-string and 6-string), two volume and two tone controls, three-way pickup-selector switch, and 3-way neck-selector switch. Other notable players include: Don Felder, Ace Frehley, Pete Townshend, Steve Howe, Alex Lifeson, John McLaughlin, Slash, and Joe Walsh.

Gibson ES-130

In 1954 Gibson introduced the ES-130 archtop guitar. It has a non-cutaway design with a single P90 pickup on a dark-stained white-bound maple body with a sunburst finished maple top. The mahogany neck has a 19-fret Brazilian rosewood fingerboard with trapezoid inlays, while the headstock has individual Kluson Deluxe tuners. Volume and tone controls are positioned between the lower f-hole and height-adjustable rosewood bridge and the strings are anchored at a trapeze tailpiece. The ES-130 was produced for only two years when it was replaced by the very similar ES-135 model.

Gibson ES-335

The ES-335, released in 1958, was the first commercially available semi-hollowbody electric guitar. While appearing to be of hollowbody construction, a solid block of wood runs through the centre of the body, beneath the pickups and bridge, creating acoustic chambers on either side. The aim was to retain the warmer tones of a hollowbody guitar while reducing feedback problems. Built to Gibson's usual high standards with maple body, mahogany neck and rosewood fingerboard, the ES-335 is popular in jazz, rock and blues music, and is most often associated with B.B. King, who has his own signature model, the B.B. King Lucille.

Gibson Explorer

The Explorer, introduced in 1958, is a radically designed guitar with an angular Z-shaped body, a sibling of the equally radical Flying V from the same year. The original run of Explorers built from korina are highly prized among collectors, especially those with the early 3+3 split headstock design instead of the more familiar "banana" shape. Over the years Gibson has released multiple variations, and the basic design has been adopted and used in modified form by many other manufacturers. Notable players include: Allen Collins from Lynyrd Skynyrd, U2's The Edge, Billy Gibbons from ZZ Top and Dave Grohl of the Foo Fighters.

Gibson Firebird

Gibson launched the Firebird in 1963. Looking like a more rounded version of the Explorer, it was designed by car designer Ray Dietrich at the invitation of Gibson president Ted McCarty. It was the first Gibson to have neck-through construction instead of a glued-in neck. In 1965 Gibson reinstated the glued-in neck and flipped over the shape (which previously looked upside-down) and issued the so-called "non-reverse" Firebird. The guitar now looked more like a Fender and prompted complaints and threats of a lawsuit from the owners. The "non-reverse" model was dropped in 1969 and the original "reverse" design was re-issued in 1972.

Gibson Flying V

Released alongside the Explorer in 1958, the Flying V was also a new modernist guitar fashioned from korina, a light-colored tonewood with properties similar to mahogany. The original mahogany prototype had been triangular in shape, like a Russian balalaika, but in a serendipitous move when a portion of wood was cut away from the rear to reduce weight, the now famous V design was born. The guitar features two humbuckers with a volume control for each, a shared tone control and a 3-way switch. Mahogany was used again for the re-issued Flying V first appearing in 1967 with a redesigned pickguard, control layout and optional vibrato.

Gibson Grabber Bass (sliding pickup)

The Grabber Bass and its sibling the Ripper were introduced in 1973, and unlike other Gibson basses both have a 34" scale and a bolt-on neck more in keeping with the designs of Fender. Built from maple (and later alder) and featuring a single pickup with volume and tone controls, these basses looked quite innocuous. However, the Grabber had an innovative feature in the shape of a sliding single coil pickup, which the player could "grab", and reposition to alter the tone. A later version of the Grabber was known as the G3 and had three non-movable pickups.

Gibson J-160E

The J-160E was Gibson's first foray into acoustic-electric guitars. The guitar is a round-shouldered non-cutaway dreadnought-sized acoustic built largely from plywood. The neck has a rosewood fingerboard with crown inlays and, unusually, joins the body at the 15th fret. Between the fingerboard and the soundhole sits a discreetly positioned uncovered P90 pickup. The lower bout of the guitar is home to volume and tone controls mounted in the guitar's top. Because of the type of pickup used, the amplified sound is more like that of a hollowbodied electric than an acoustic, but this didn't stop both John Lennon and George Harrison of The Beatles extensively using this guitar.

> *"I don't understand why some people will only accept a guitar if it has an instantly recognizable guitar sound. Finding ways to use the same guitar people have been using for 50 years to make sounds that no one has heard before is truly what gets me off."*
>
> - Jeff Beck

Gibson Les Paul

Truly one of the giants, the Les Paul was inspired by Lester William Polsfuss (Les Paul) in the 1950s, but later editions have paid homage to more modern musicians such as the version created for rock legend Slash. Used by practically every rock star since its conception, the Les Paul is not necessarily the oldest electric guitar, but it is definitely one of the most famous in the world. The Les Paul typically has a solid mahogany body embellished by a carved maple wood top, which has changed very little from its introduction. This is the guitar that defined an entire generation of music.

Gibson Les Paul Signature Semi Goldtop

When the whole concept behind the Les Paul guitar is that it has a solid body, what is a semi-hollowbodied guitar doing bearing the Les Paul name? The Signature, made briefly during the mid 1970s, is a semi-hollowbody double cutaway guitar featuring two low-impedance humbuckers. Both the top and back are arched maple, with sides of walnut and a mahogany neck. The 22-fret bound fingerboard is rosewood with pearl trapezoid inlays. The three-way switch, two volumes and two tones are laid out as you'd expect on a Les Paul. Tobacco sunburst and goldtop finishes were both available, with the goldtop looking particularly stunning.

Gibson TG-25 Tenor Guitar

Gibson's first tenor guitars were introduced in the late 1920s, when any guitar model in their catalogue could be made available as a tenor by special order. The TG-25, made between 1962 and 1971, is a tenor version of the B-25. It has mahogany back and sides and a spruce top with a sunburst or natural finish. To accommodate the shorter scale length of the tenor guitar, the bridge is noticeably nearer to the soundhole than it would be on its six-string counterpart.

Gibson Skylark EH-500 Lap Steel

The Gibson Skylark EH-500 is a student model lap steel, first introduced in 1956 and available until 1968. Built from korina, it has an asymmetrical body with a bevel carved around the top edge. The fingerboard is black with cream numeric open block markers. A rather shapeless headstock houses three-on-a-plate Kluson Deluxe tuners with black plastic buttons and a raised Gibson logo. A slanted singlecoil pickup, volume, tone, covered bridge and output jack all sit on a chromed metal plate at the base of the body.

Lucille
L5
BASS
FREQUENCY
MIDRANGE
TREBLE
MULTI FILTER
REVERB
100W 212
COMPRESSOR

Gibson SG

The younger brother of the Les Paul was developed in 1961, as sales of the Les Paul were dropping and Gibson panic-designed a sequel to boost sales. The new body style and thinner cutaway horns make the upper frets easier to reach, but the design did not impress Les Paul who asked to have his name removed from this version. The improvements may have made for a more comfortable play, but its older brother will always steal the limelight. Notable players include: Tony Iommi of Black Sabbath, Robbie Krieger of The Doors and Angus Young of AC/DC.

"My guitar is not a thing. It is an extension of myself. It is who I am."
- Joan Jett

Gibson Thunderbird Bass

The Thunderbird Bass was introduced in 1963 at the same time as its guitar sibling, the Firebird, and was another design by Ray Dietrich. It is of neck-through construction and has a 34" scale, equal to that of Fender's basses. Two versions were available with one and two pickups. The body shape is popularly known as "reverse" style as it has a noticeably longer horn on the treble side, which gives it an upside-down look. Gibson revamped the design in 1966 and "non-reverse" Thunderbirds were available until being discontinued three years later. The original "reverse" styling was reissued from 1976 to 1979, and again in 1987 and is still in production. (see picture below)

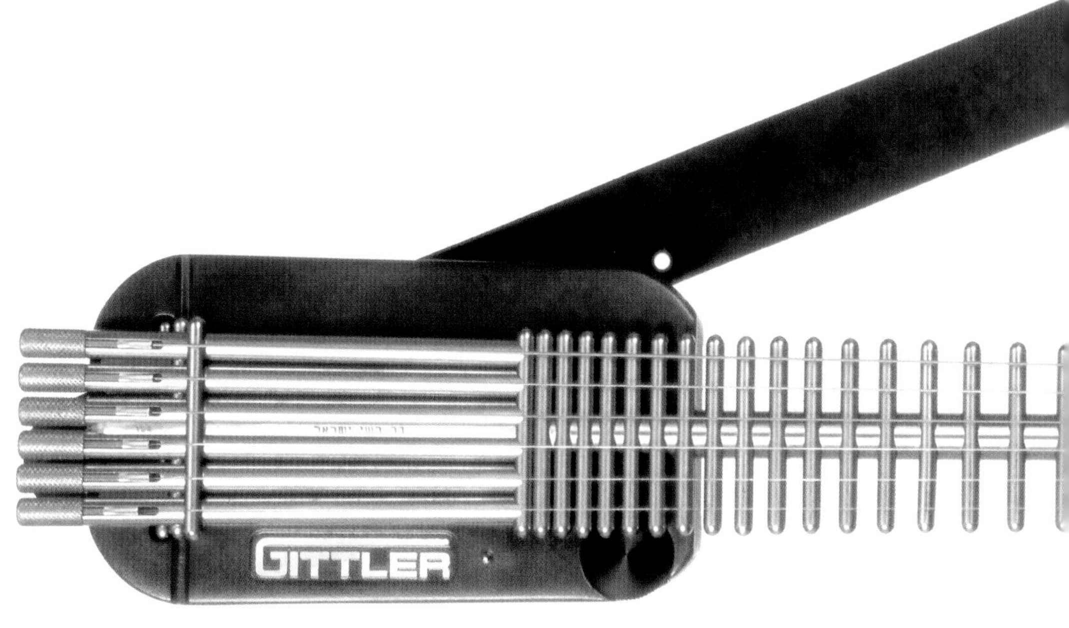

Girl Brand

Girl Brand guitars are playable one-off works of art by luthier Chris Larsen of Arizona, based loosely on the Tele shape. Bodies are of a hollow-construction and formed from an aluminium rim supporting top and back plates, which can be made from materials such as formica, rusted steel, plastic laminates, street signs, etc. Notable one-offs include: Hollywood Girl with Marilyn Monroe inlayed fingerboard; Radio Girl with radio dials set into the top; and Sushi Girl with a plate of plastic sushi behind a window in the guitar's top!

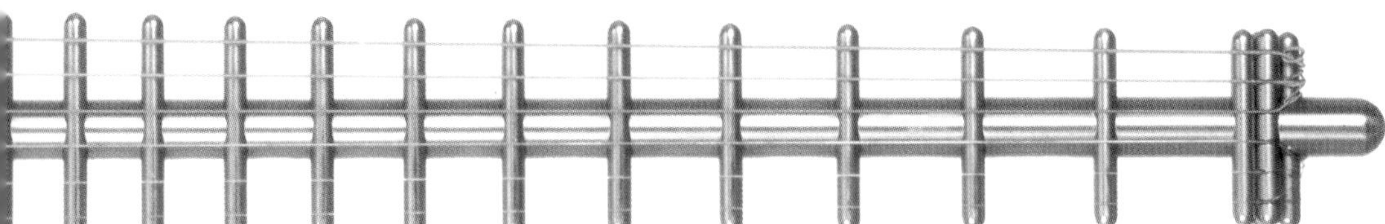

"I don't read music. I don't write it. So I wander around on the guitar until something starts to present itself."
- James Taylor

Gittler

The Gittler is a minimalistic guitar created by Allan Gittler in the late 1970s to early 1980s. Often likened to a fishbone, the guitar has no proper neck as such. It is made from a stainless steel rod with smaller stainless steel bars arranged along its length acting as frets. The body section simply consists of six rods aligned one under each string, with each containing an individual pickup. Each of the strings then has its own output and can be sent to separate channels on a mixer or to different amps. The guitar is headless with fine tuners at its base.

Godin A11 Glissentar

The Godin Glissentar is an 11-string fretless nylon-strung electro-acoustic guitar, inspired by the Arabian oud, a fretless lute that is still popular in Armenia and Egypt today. Strings are arranged in paired courses, with the exception of the lowest bass which is a single string as on the oud itself. The use of standard guitar tuning gives guitarists a familiar base from which to experiment with eastern sounds. The fretless fingerboard also allows for microtonal playing by those adventurous enough to attempt it.

Godin Acousticaster

Godin Guitars, founded by Robert Godin, are a forward-thinking manufacturer of guitars based in Quebec, Canada. The Acousticaster is Godin's thin-bodied Tele-shaped electro-acoustic model. It has a 25" scale length on a precisely fitting rock maple neck with 22-fret rosewood fingerboard. The two-chambered silver leaf maple body has a solid spruce top concealing a Godin innovation: eighteen tuned metal tines are mounted beneath the bridge, adding resonance and creating the unique sound of the guitar.

"It was my 16th birthday - my mom and dad gave me my Goya classical guitar that day. I sat down, wrote this song, and I just knew that that was the only thing I could ever really do - write songs and sing them to people."
- Stevie Nicks

Godin

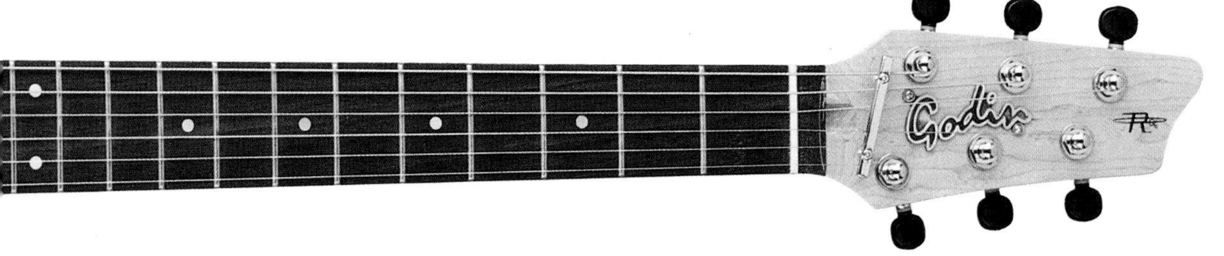
Godin

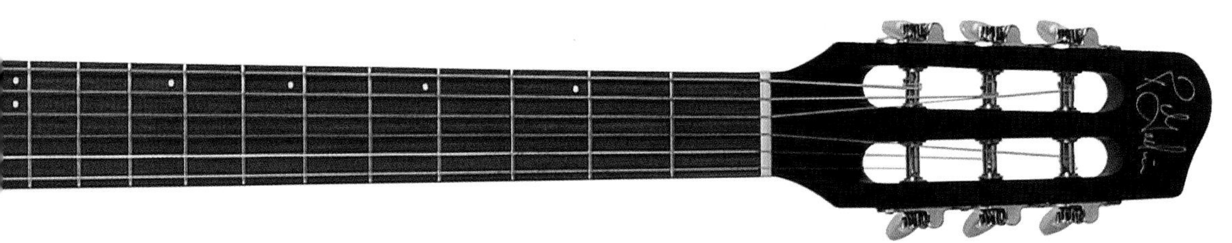

Godin Radiator

The Radiator is Godin's entry-level guitar but is still a professional quality instrument with no corners cut in its construction. The scale length is an easy to manage Gibson-like 24". The guitar has a chambered silver leaf maple body and bolt-on rock maple neck with maple or rosewood fingerboard. All 24 frets are easily accessible thanks to the deep cutaway on the treble side of the body. Pickups are two of Godin's own low-noise single coils each with its own volume control allowing for a wide range of tones to be selected.

Goldbug Hombre

The limited edition Hombre celebrates America's "Old West". Metal hardware is handcrafted in solid sterling silver in Delavan, Wisconsin, while control knobs are Spencer 56-50 cartridge casings. The guitar is constructed with a long tenon joint glued-in neck, and body and neck are of South African mahogany with solid walnut carved top finished in hand-rubbed varnish simulating the stock of an antique rifle. Accessories include a custom-made cartridge belt guitar strap, medicine bag made by a Native American bead artist and guitar case made to resemble an antique firearms shipping crate. Behind the bridge is a holster designed to fit a small derringer - the guitar comes with a small non-functional replica.

"At the point where I'm trying to force something and it's not happening, and I'm getting frustrated with, say, writing a poem, I can go and pick up the brushes and start painting. At the point where the painting seems to not be going anywhere, I go and pick up the guitar." - Joni Mitchell

Goldfish Guitars Orange Clownfish

This is a guitar for the younger players and fans of "Finding Nemo". The Juba Clownfish is a lightweight short-scale guitar at 22". Shaped like a fish and finished in clownfish colors, the guitar has a 20-fret rosewood fingerboard, single-coil pickup and a built-in amp and speaker with a volume knob running off a 9-volt battery. It's designed to appeal to children while adults and teenagers may like to use it as a travel guitar.

Gold Tone ES-Banjitar

Is it a Tele or is it a banjo? The ES-Banjitar has a Tele-shaped solid body with a hollow sound chamber mounted with a banjo head. It has two pickups, one in the usual Tele neck pickup position and the other under the banjo head. Body and neck are made of maple with a rosewood fingerboard, with white binding on the neck and snowflake fingerboard inlays. It's a quality electric banjo for players familiar with the guitar, all in a familiar six-string package. (see picture opposite)

Goodall Traditional Rosewood Baritone Acoustic

Goodall Guitars are built in California by James Goodall who completed his first guitar in 1972 with no previous woodworking experience. Today he crafts the incredibly exacting, high-class acoustic guitars built to deliver a robust, three dimensional sound character. The Traditional Rosewood Baritone has rosewood back and sides with a bear claw Sitka spruce top and maple binding. It is a round-shouldered guitar with a 28" scale which allows the guitar to be tuned a whole step down using regular medium-gauge strings. With heavier strings it can be pitched as low as B.

Gold Tone

Gordon Smith GS 1.5

Built in the UK, Gordon Smith guitars have long been the well-guarded secret of many discerning guitarists and those in the know, offering exceptional build quality, workhorse-like reliability, good looks and a very reasonable price tag. The GS series are reminiscent of Gibson's Les Paul Junior guitars and are available with different pickup and hardware options and a choice of single or double cutaways. The GS 1.5 features mahogany body and neck, 22-fret rosewood fingerboard and a pair of Gordon Smith pickups: one single-coil and one humbucker. (see picture opposite and below)

Gottschall Funnelbody double-sided guitar

Germany's Gottschall Guitars offer a number of interesting innovations in acoustic guitar design. One such innovation is the Funnelbody. Viewed from the side, the guitar is clearly wedge-shaped, with its widest point at the neck joint. This shape acts like that of a speaker, projecting the sound from the bridge, along the inside of the body and out through sound ports located in the twin cutaways either side of the neck. The double-sided guitar works on the same principles with two necks back-to-back. One side of the guitar is a steel string and the other is nylon string. It is two guitars in one, but less cumbersome than a conventional doubleneck.

Goulding Aluminum Guitars

Anthony Goulding of Goulding Guitars in the UK builds precision-made hollowbody electric guitars, each machined from two solid billets of aluminium and exquisitely hand finished. The neck is created from a single billet of aluminum and has an ebony fingerboard with optional inlay work, while a second billet is machined from the rear to create the hollow body. Hardware, bridges, pickup surrounds and knobs are all hard-crafted from aluminum, brass, gold-plated brass or stainless steel. There are many finish options from chrome-plated to brightly colored anodized finishes. Choice of pickups, piezo transducers and Bigsby vibrato are all optional.

GOULDING
Bigsby

Goya Rangemaster

The Goya brand name appeared on guitars imported into the US by the Hershman Musical Instrument Company of New York. The solidbody Rangemaster guitars, produced between 1965 and 1969, were of Italian origin featuring two split singlecoil pickups and the usual pushbutton controls popular on Italian guitars of that period. These guitars were possibly made by Italy's Polverini Brothers, although the vibrato has been identified as being by Hagström of Sweden. To confuse things further, the Rangemaster name was also applied to semihollow electric guitars, including a 12-string, which bore no resemblance to the solidbodies other than having the same pickups and pushbuttons.

Greenfield Guitars Don Alder Model G4

Greenfield Guitars, crafted by Michael Greenfield in his Montreal workshop, incorporate modern techniques and design innovations. Exotic tonewoods and well-seasoned soundboards are selected to achieve specific tonal results. The Don Alder G4 acoustic strikingly uses the Novax Fanned Fret system, giving the guitar a scale length of 27" on the bass side and 25" on the treble side. The ergonomics of the system places the left hand in a more natural, comfortable playing position with much less physical stress. The longer scale of the bass strings gives increased clarity to bass notes, and is especially recommended for players who use DADGAD or C tunings.

Greenfield Guitars Nylon String Model C3

The nylon-strung C3 model from Greenfield Guitars is described as a wolf in sheep's clothing. Its most obvious departure from traditional classical guitar design is in its placing of the soundhole on the treble side of the top. It also features a secondary soundport on the upper rim facing the player. Less obvious features are a double top and concentric circular acoustic radiators developed with acoustic physicist Dr. Evan B. Davis, PhD. Additionally, the underside of the top is braced with an asymmetric, elongated fan. All this adds up to make an instrument of exceptional volume, projection and clarity.

Gretsch Bo Diddley

The late Bo Diddley's rectangular guitar was his trademark. The G6138 is a replica of the guitar Gretsch built for him in 1958. Its unusual body shape aside, the guitar has the usual appointments you'd expect from Gretsch: two Filtertron pickups with a volume for each plus master tone, master volume and 3-way switch. The semihollow body, finished in Firebird red, is constructed from alder with a 6-ply maple top. The neck is made from 3-piece rock maple and has a 22-fret ebonized rosewood fingerboard with pearl inlays. This is the perfect guitar for twanging out those infectious riffs and that Bo Diddley beat.

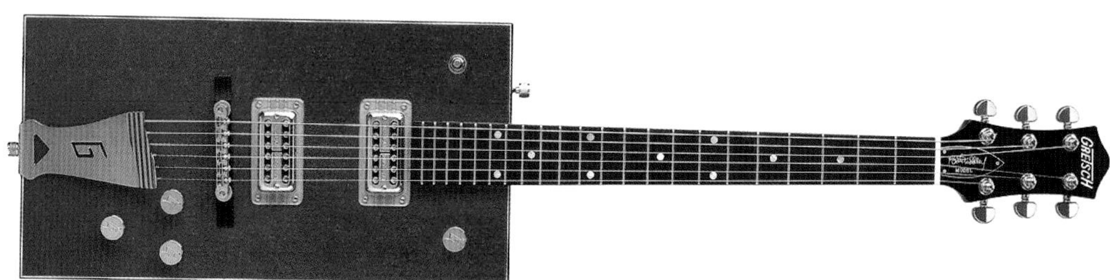

Gretsch G6120RHH Reverend Horton Heat

With its unique combination of 1955-style Gretsch Western motifs and 1958 pickups and controls, the G6120RHH guitar, designed for Jim Heath (aka "Reverend Horton Heat), may look traditional but is a hybrid. The single cutaway archtop hollowbody is made from laminated maple with a two-piece maple neck. The 22-fret fingerboard is inlaid with aged vintage Western block markers of cactus, steerheads and fences. Aged binding is used throughout, and the headstock has a stained curly maple overlay with an inlaid pearloid steerhead and Gretsch logo. Other details such as the "G" brand in the guitar's top, oversized f-holes and aluminium Bigsby make this a mighty fine rocking guitar.

Gretsch Rancher

In an orange-red Western maple stain displaying a G-brand on the body and with a triangular soundhole, this big-bodied jumbo acoustic could only be a Gretsch. The laminated maple body is a whole 17" wide with a laminated spruce top. The neck is 3-piece maple and has a 21-fret neck with Western motif pearloid inlay markers. The headstock carries the Gretsch logo and steerhead motif. With gold hardware, bound body and fingerboard, this guitar just begs you to play some cowboy songs on it around the campfire.

Gretsch
Synchromatic

Gretsch White Falcon

This is the Cadillac of guitars. Originally created in 1955 to improve upon the Gibson Super 400, instead the makers created an icon in its own right used by John Frusciante, Matthew Ashman and Johnny Marr who no doubt chose this instrument for its unique sound and appearance. Punching through nicely for lead but managing with a huge bass for rhythm, this is a guitar that will get you noticed. (picture right and on opposite page)

Grosh Guitars ElectraJet

Set in the foothills of the Rocky Mountains in Broomfield, Colorado, Grosh Guitars build high-end boutique instruments. The ElectraJet is an original but vintage-looking design that somehow seems to meld together elements of Jaguar, Strat and Tele. Crafted from "Tap Matched" old-growth tonewoods to ensure a harmonically rich, dynamic and acoustically alive instrument, the ElectraJet has a Tele-like slab body with Jaguar-like offset waist and upper horn. Hardware includes two P90 pickups with volume, tone and 3-way switch, plus Gotoh 6-screw 510T bridge with push-in tremolo arm. The guitar is capable of fat, thick and heavy tones like the very best of them while maintaining clarity and harmonic complexity.

Guild B-302 Bass

The Guild B-302 was produced between 1977 and 1980 and was the twin pickup companion to the B-301 bass and the S-300 guitar. With a design looking like a smaller-bodied relative of the Rickerbacker 4001, the B-302 had a 34" scale length, set neck and was built from mahogany. The rosewood fingerboard had 20 frets, and a fretless version was also available. An ash-bodied, maple neck version designated the B-302A was available from 1978-1981. Notable players include David Goldflies of The Allman Brothers Band and Derek Holt of Climax Blues Band.

Guild DE 500 Duane Eddy

The Guild Duane Eddy model was based on the Guild T-500, which itself was a slimmer version of the Stuart 500 archtop. Guild issued two Duane Eddy models in 1960, the DE-400 and deluxe DE-500, affording Eddy the distinction of being the first rock and roll artist with his own signature guitar. The DE-500 is a single cutaway hollowbodied guitar with set neck, twin DeArmond pickups and Bigsby vibrato. The bound body is constructed from mahogany and the neck is three-ply maple/mahogany/maple and has a medium to thick profile and ebony fingerboard. Surprisingly, given Eddy's big bassy sound, the guitar is thin-bodied, weighing just 7.10lbs.

"It is the most delightful thing that ever happens to me, when I hear something coming out of my guitar and out of my mouth that wasn't there before."
- James Taylor

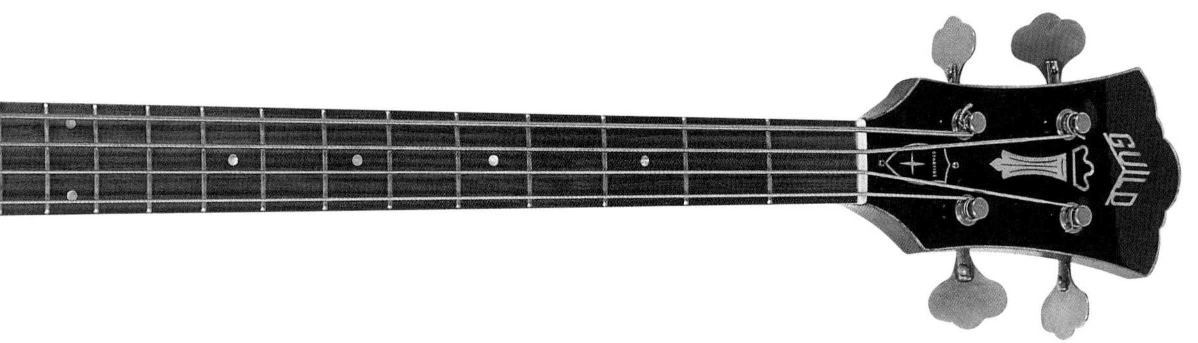

Guild F-412 Jumbo 12-string

The F-412 is one of the all-time classic acoustic 12-string guitars. Beloved by both gigging players and studio musicians alike, the guitar has a reputation for terrific volume and outstanding sound definition. Designed in the late 1960s, the body dimensions of this jumbo are 17" wide, 21" long, and 4.8" deep. The arched back and sides are maple, and the top is solid Sitka spruce. A sibling model, the F-512, has back and sides made of rosewood. Modern reissues are available with the D-TAR pickup system, which combines a thin, piezo under-saddle transducer with an 18-volt, low-noise, high-input impedance preamp.

Guild Starfire IV

The Starfire IV is a double cutaway semi-hollowbodied guitar with a center block to reduce feedback, as pioneered on Gibson's ES-335. The 24" scale guitar has two SD1 humbuckers, Guild adjust-o-matic bridge and harp tailpiece. Top, back and sides are of either laminated maple or mahogany, while the neck is 3-ply mahogany with a rosewood fretboard. It first went into production in 1963, and was re-designed in 1967 when the neck/body join changed from the 16th to 18th fret. Some models were available with optional stereo circuitry. Notable players include Buddy Guy, Lightnin' Hopkins and John Mayer. (see picture of Slash playing a Guild doubleneck on opposite page)

Marshall
GUILD
GUILD

Guild X100 Blade Runner

The Guild X100 Blade Runner dates back to 1984, when 95 examples were built. The guitar was likened to an Explorer with holes in the body; the holes were strategically positioned to reduce weight and to increase sustain and tone in a design patented by David Andrews Guitar Research and licensed to Guild. In 1985 Schecter Guitars issued the similar-looking Genesis model (allegedly copied from a fuzzy picture in a New York trade magazine), and in 2009 Gibson released the Holy Explorer and put an inflated price tag on it. Joe Perry of Aerosmith plays a Guild X100 Blade Runner in the video to “Walk This Way” with Run DMC.

Guyatone Doubleneck Lap Steel

Guyatone was a Japanese company that produced a range of effects pedals and some budget lap steel guitars in the Fender Stringmaster tradition. The doubleneck model has two 8-string necks, each with a single pickup and rudimentary bridge. The two fingerboards are made of printed perspex with circle, triangle, square and diamond position markers. A metal plate between the necks carries volume and tone controls along with a neck selector switch and output jack. The guitar has legs that screw into its underside and for that reason should more accurately be called a console guitar.

Gibson

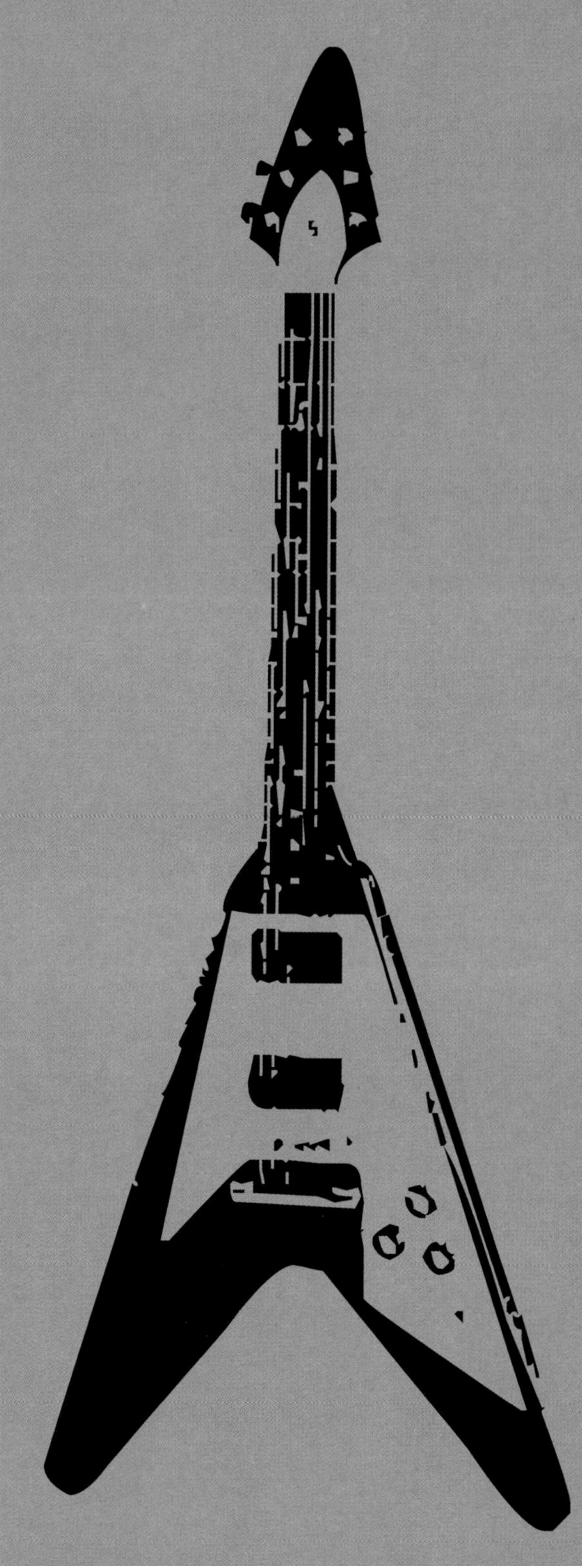

Hagström 8-string Bass

Hagström of Sweden produced the H8, the first 8-string bass, between 1967 and 1969. It was the bass equivalent of the 12-string guitar, with strings paired into four courses; each pair tuned an octave apart. The bass is perfect for use in a power trio with guitar and drums, functioning effectively as bass and rhythm guitar. The H8 has a short 30.75" scale, offset double cutaway body, bolt-on maple neck, white-bound rosewood fretboard with pearloid dot inlays, two singlecoil pickups and switches for low, high, tone and mute. Notable users included Noel Redding, Jimi Hendrix and Mike Rutherford. (see picture opposite)

Hagström/Goya Standard (Glitter Top)

The Hagström Standard (imported to the US under the Goya brand) was manufactured from 1958 to 1962 and is a guitar with a flamboyant aesthetic. The top of this guitar is usually covered in glitter while back and sides are resplendent in pearloid vinyl. Pickups are mounted on panel with a line of pushbuttons on the bass side and a pickguard on the treble side. The fingerboard is made of clear plexiglass mounted over more pearl, as is the headstock. The Standard, initially known as the Sweetone, has two singlecoil pickups (a humbucker-equipped model was known as the Deluxe). The neck is reinforced with aluminium around the truss rod, and vibrato-equipped models were offered towards the end of the guitar's production.

Hagström Super Swede

The Super Swede is an attractive single cutaway guitar in the Les Paul tradition with a rounded lower cutaway and a Fender-like 25.5" scale. The body is made of mahogany with a carved maple top and flamed maple cap, while the set mahogany neck has a 22-fret Resinator fingerboard with pearl block position markers. Pickups are Hagstöm's own custom 58 humbuckers and controls are a Les Paul-like 3-way switch, two volumes and two tones with the addition of a coil tap switch for singlecoil sounds. Hagström's own brand tuners, mounted on an unusual, asymmetrical headstock, top off a very fine guitar. (see picture opposite)

Hamer Talladega

The Talladega is one of Hamer's top of the line custom-built guitars. The concept behind it was, in Jol Dantzig's words, "to balance a warm-toned chambered mahogany body with a maple neck as a way of getting both an airy snap and a rich fundamental." The Talladega uses specially designed singlecoil pickups by Seymour Duncan to capture overtones and help with string separation. The guitar itself has an ivoroid bound mahogany body with an arched chambered curly maple top. The neck is maple with a rosewood fingerboard, and other hardware includes a Hamer Sustain Block bridge and TonePros Keystone tuners. The guitar is flawlessly finished in amberburst.

Harmony Professional H1252 Hawaiian Guitar

Harmony was founded in 1892 by Wilhelm Schultz, going on to become the largest producer of musical instruments in the US by the 1930s. The Harmony Professional H1252 Hawaiian Guitar, circa 1940, would at the time have been one of their top of the range models. It is a guitar designed for playing lap-style and so has a square backed neck. The body is a double bound "extra auditorium" style (15" wide) with a spruce top and flamed mahogany back and sides. The square neck is mahogany with a bound Brazilian rosewood fretboard inlaid with diamonds, dots and blocks. The guitar is topped off with a pearloid "Harmony Professional" headstock.

Hallmark Swept-Wing

The claim that the 1960s Swept-Wing could be mistaken for a Mosrite guitar is not too far from the truth. Joe Hall, original founder of Hallmark, had worked in Semie Moseley's workshop near Bakersfield, California in the late 50s. Bob Bogle, bassist for the Ventures, brought the basic Swept-Wing design to him. Hallmark took a small run of finished guitars to the 1967 NAMM show, but unfortunately they were not a hit and the company folded shortly thereafter. The few guitars that were produced gained almost legendary status after a Guitar World magazine feature - 40 years after the event the Swept-Wing was re-issued.

Hamer Chaparral 12-string Bass

The 12-string bass has the strings arranged into four courses with three strings per course - one bass string and two octaves – resulting in a bass with even more twang. Tom Petersson of Cheap Trick suggested the idea to Hamer Guitars designer Jol Dantzig who thought there would be too much tension on the neck. A compromise was reached and a 10-string was built with just the D and G strings tripled. It worked beautifully so they decided to go for the twelve. Since then 12-string basses have been produced by over 30 manufacturers. The Chaparral is a 34" scale 12-string bass currently in production at Hamer.

Harmos Americana

Looking at the Americana lap steel guitar you might be forgiven for thinking it was a model spacecraft from a science fiction TV series; Harmos Guitars from Minnesota specialize in building 21st century carbon fibre space frame guitars. The heart of the instrument - the space frame - is formed from struts that geometrically intertwine tetrahedra and octahedra together into a 3-dimensional design pattern known as the Octet Truss. The structure is highly efficient with natural frequencies yielding clear, transparent fundamentals and harmonics. The carbon fiber allows for long sustain times, transmission of string energy, and has great strength.

Harmos MatraX

The MatraX is a six-string electric guitar with a body largely composed of the same carbon fiber space frame as used on Harmos lap steels. This 3-dimensional design makes for an extra light, extra strong guitar with excellent sustain. The design incorporates wood alongside the carbon fiber, such as the maple neck, to add another dimension to the fundamental resonance of the guitar. Guitars are available in both headed and headless versions. It is a comfortable and well balanced guitar, and is said to have a crunchy low end, woody mid-ranges and a full sounding, very precise high end.

J.C. Harper Vegas Vulcan

J.C. Harper has famously built guitars for members of Blue Oyster Cult. The Vegas Vulcan is a design that looks like a synthesis of a Flying V and an Explorer, and is an updated version of a guitar played by Buck Dharma of Blue Oyster Cult in the 1970s. Body and neck are made of mahogany with a 22-fret mother of pearl inlaid rosewood fingerboard on a 24" scale. Pickups are DiMarzio PAF and PAF Pro at the neck and bridge respectively. Other hardware includes Grover Rotomatic tuners and tune-o-matic bridge with a stop tailpiece.

Hembry Custom Doubleneck Jazz bass

Hembry Guitars are based in Shelton, Washington, and built in the workshop of Scott Hembry. Specializing in one-off guitars, Scott has built more than his fair share of doublenecks, which have included several double-necked Jazz basses. The body is faithful to the Fender design but is nearly twice as large. The top neck is fretted while the lower is fretless, and the controls - located on the traditional plate on the lower part of the body - are kept simple with individual volumes for each neck and a three-way pickup selector. Another of Hembry's double Jazz Basses marries together 4-string and 8-string necks.

Hoffman Harp Guitar

Charlie Hoffman, a former lawyer, has been building and repairing guitars since 1970. With a workshop in Minneapolis, Hoffman offers eight basic acoustic guitar models from Dreadnought to Piccolo. The most unusual of these is the Harp Guitar. When a customer brought in a Dyer Harp Guitar with the back off for repair, Hoffman was able to closely study its interior construction for reference when building his own version. The resulting guitar, based on the Dyer but with Hoffman's own design elements, has a regular six-string neck and five sub-bass strings on the elongated upper arm of the body. The harp strings are said to have an almost piano-like tone.

Hofner Artist Bass

The Hofner Artist Bass dates from 1962 and has an offset body shape inspired by the Fender Jazz Bass, with a 30" scale. Two "toastrack" pickups are set as far apart as the design will allow and each has a volume and tone control. The body is made of abachi, which is essentially a hard version of balsawood, and some examples have a mahogany veneer applied to front and back. The neck is made of a single piece of maple and is clear lacquered, and has a rosewood fingerboard with Hofner's pearloid strip markers spanning the width of the board.

Hofner Verithin

The aptly-named Verithin has a hollow body of only 1". It dates from 1960 and was distributed in the UK by Selmer. Elsewhere in the world it was known as the 4574. The design resembles the Gibson 335 but lacks the solid centre block. The shallow body depth may have been Hofner's own attempt at reducing feedback. The maple body has a laminated spruce top with bookmatched flamed maple veneers on the back and is fully bound, including the f-holes. The neck is three-ply maple/beech/maple with a rosewood fingerboard. Pickups were initially singlecoils but switched to humbuckers in 1963. A stereo model was offered but decent examples are rare. (see picture opposite)

Hofner Violin Bass

Germany's Hofner guitars hit the big time when their Model 500/1 bass was selected by The Beatles' Paul McCartney as his instrument of choice. In 1961, McCartney was relegated to bass-playing duties following the departure of Stuart Sutcliffe from The Beatles. He bought his first "violin bass" for £30 in Hamburg, choosing it because the symmetrical shape appealed to him as a left-handed player. The design dates from 1956 and is a hollowbodied model, even though there are no soundholes. This and its 30" scale length make it an easy-to-play, lightweight instrument with a rich tone.

Hohner The Artist

Once considered a "copy" guitar, "The Artist" has become much sought after mainly through being one of Prince's favourite guitars, his being from the Hohner Professional series. Styled after the Fender Telecaster, this model was originally built by H.S. Andersen in Japan and called the Madcat before being licensed to Hohner. The body is made from Californian maple with a center strip of walnut and brown pearloid binding. The bridge pickup and bridge sit on a plate made from the same material as the tortoiseshell pickguard. The neck is Canadian maple and early models had a Fender Tele-shaped headstock. Pickups are Hohner Professional singlecoils. (see picture below)

Hopf Saturn

The Hopf Saturn 63 - as its name suggests - dates back to 1963 and was made in Germany. The body is maple and has a thick top of spruce and features two unusually shaped soundholes on the bass side of the body. These are bound in metal piping as is the top edge of the guitar. The Hopf patented "Everstraight" multi-laminate neck has a rosewood fingerboard and 20 frets. The guitar has two powerful singlecoil pickups and the sound is said to be very Gretsch-like. The guitar was re-issued in 2006 by Eastwood Guitars.

Hutchins "The Beast" 6-neck guitar

Hutchins Guitars, based in the UK, is a relatively new company with a range of retro-styled guitars and basses produced in the Far East. In what was probably a publicity stunt to promote the brand name, Hutchins went one further than Cheap Trick's Rick Nielsen with his five-necked Hamer, by making a limited edition six-necked guitar. The necks are, from top to bottom: 12-string guitar, 6-string guitar with tremolo, 5-string bass, 4-string bass, 7-string guitar with tremolo, and 6-string hardtail guitar. The guitar is reportedly extremely heavy and it is doubtful that the lower necks are actually reachable but it is a remarkable instrument, nonetheless.

Hutchins

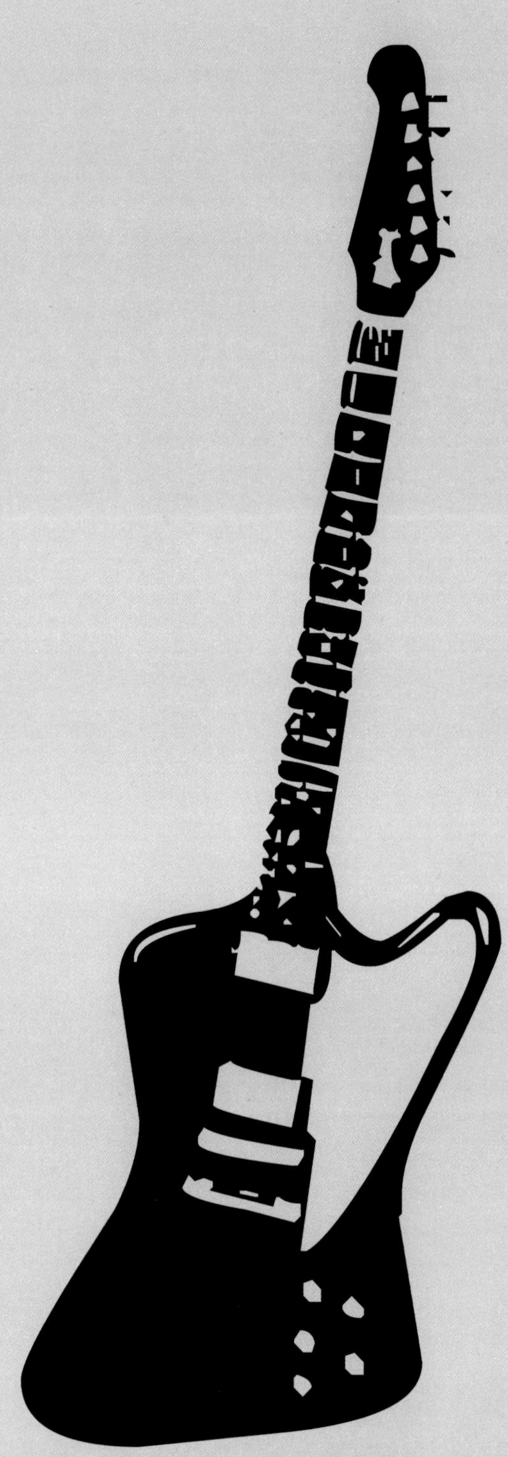

他力本
TAMA

Ibanez Artwood Twin Doubleneck

Handcrafted in Japan in the 1970s, the Artwood Twin Doubleneck is truly a luxuriously appointed guitar. The body is solid natural ash with twin set necks in maple and rosewood 22-fret fingerboards, each inlaid with a "Tree of Life" design in ivory, pearl and abalone. Pickups are Super 70 humbuckers wired to give a full range of humbucker, single coil and out-of-phase sounds. Control-wise there are two tones, two volumes, master volume and 3-way switches for pickup selection and neck selection. The bridges are tune-o-matics with brass sustain blocks beneath, and the Ibanez Deluxe tuners have pearl buttons. The guitar was famously used by Gerry Beckley of America.

Ibanez Iceman

Ibanez is a guitar brand owned by Hoshino Gakki of Japan. The Iceman was originally produced from 1975 to 1983 and was the first original design for Ibanez after having previously copied Fender, Gibson and Rickenbacker designs. Several different models of the Iceman were produced with set necks, bolt-on necks, different woods and pickup options. An intriguing early model has a triple coil sliding pickup that can be moved between neck and bridge positions to access different tones. Greco Guitars of Japan also produced the same guitars, which they named Mirage, for the Japanese market. Notable players include Steve Miller and Paul Stanley. (see picture opposite)

Ibanez JEM 20th Anniversary Acrylic

The JEM series of guitars have been manufactured by Ibanez since 1987. Working from the specifications of Steve Vai, the guitars were designed by Joe Despagni. Built very much in the superstrat mold, they are usually very easily recognized by the integral "monkeygrip" in the body. The JEM 20th Anniversary model is perhaps the most flamboyant of them all, with a body made from clear acrylic with random streaks of color running through it. It also lights up inside and glows eerily. Other features are three DiMarzio pickups, EdgePro tremolo and tree-of-life fingerboard inlay.

Ibanez Joe Satriani Signature JS1600

The JS series from Ibanez is endorsed by none other than the master of instrumental rock himself, Joe Satriani, and the 20th Anniversary Signature model, the JS1600, debuted at the NAMM 2008 show. The mahogany body is highly contoured with no hard edges and is very comfortable to play. A combination of a 25" scale length and DiMarzio pickups provides wide dynamic range and versatility, while the fast maple JS Prestige neck with rosewood fingerboard are complemented by an Edge Pro hardtail bridge. Most strikingly, a premium silver finish adorns the body. (see Joe Satriani with his Ibanez. opposite)

Ibanez Talman TCM60BBU Acoustic

Ibanez's range of double cutaway acoustic Talman guitars is designed for the guitarist who wants the sound and tonality of an acoustic with the comfort and playing ease of an electric. The TCM60BBU has mahogany neck, back and sides, with a spruce top featuring a heart-shaped soundhole. Rosewood is used for the 20-fret fingerboard and bridge, while the nut and saddle are of Ivorex II for extra strength, durability and transmission of tone. The Talman also features an AP2 magnetic pickup between the soundhole and fingerboard and has an on-board pre-amp with 2-band EQ.

Ibanez Universe 7-string

First appearing in 1990, the Ibanez Universe has the distinction of being the world's first production model, modern 7-string electric guitar, and like the Ibanez JEM series that it closely resembles, it is endorsed by Steve Vai. Bodies are of basswood with bolt-on necks of maple or wenge, and fingerboards are rosewood and occasionally maple. The guitar features three DiMarzio Blade II pickups in an H-S-H formation, and an Ibanez Edge Pro 7 tremolo. Finishes have included the now famous multi-colored "swirl" designs by About Time Designs.

Doug Irwin "Tiger"

Tiger belonged to Jerry Garcia of the Grateful Dead, and was built by Doug Irwin, a former Alembic employee. Cocabola, maple, vermillion and flame maple are layered in an Alembic-style "hippie sandwich" and the top and edges are detailed with brass binding. The eponymous Tiger can be seen on the battery cover behind the bridge. It has a DiMarzio SDS-1 Strat-style pickup in the neck, and DiMarzio Super IIs as the middle and bridge pickups. The neck and bridge pickups both share a tone control, while the middle pickup has its own tone. Pickup output goes via a pre-amp to an onboard effect loop which allowed Garcia to have full volume going to his effects while controlling the output volume from the guitar.

Isana Black Real Acoustic Guitar

Isana was a German guitar manufacturer founded by Ignas Sandner and in the 1960s produced a range of solidbodies. However, the most famous Isana guitar is a black single-cutaway archtop acoustic guitar owned by Elvis Presley while serving in the U.S. Army in Germany in 1958-1960. The guitar features unique-shaped f-holes, pearloid headstock, pickguard and block fretboard position markers and was fitted with a floating pickup. In October 2006, an Isana Black Pearl guitar once owned by Elvis was put up for auction, but it is not known if this was the exact same guitar he was photographed playing in Germany. With a reserve of $150,000 it failed to sell.

Italia Maranello Bass

The singlecut glitter-finished Maranello Bass looks like a solidbody from the 1960s but is in fact a modern instrument from Italia Guitars, designed to combine retro styling with modern playability. Italia Guitars, based in the UK, are designed by Trevor Wilkinson and manufactured in South Korea. Beneath the glitter, the body of the Maranello is agathis, the bolt-on neck is hard maple and the fingerboard is rosewood. The pickups are two Wilkinson bass humbuckers, while the one tone and two volume controls plus angled output jack are on a plastic oval panel. Notable users include Nicky Wire of the Manic Street Preachers.

Italia Mondial Classic

The Mondial Classic is another retro-themed guitar from Italia Guitars. It features an agathis chambered body with an Acousti-Glass top, and a wooden bridge with a piezo pickup alongside a pair of regular humbuckers. The electrics are comprised of separate volumes for magnetic and piezo pickups, one tone control, two EQ knobs and a three-way toggle. The piezo pickup does not give an authentic approximation of an acoustic guitar tone, but serves as an additional tonal element that can be mixed with the magnetic pickups. (see another Italia model pictured below)

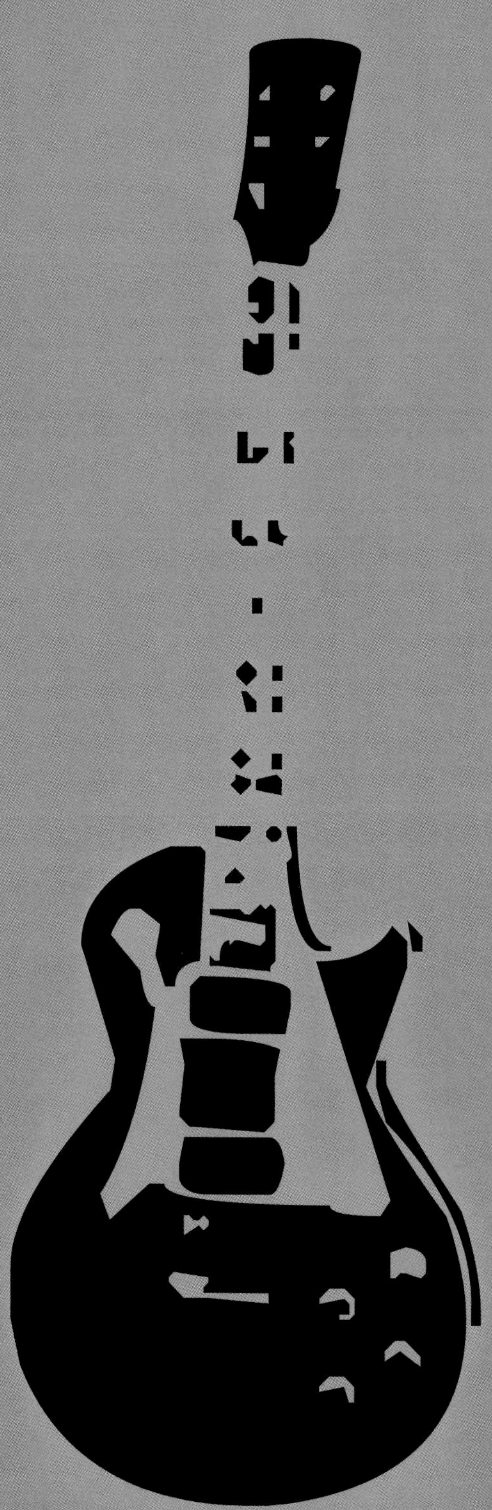

Jackson DK2 Dinky

Jackson Guitars, founded by Grover Jackson, will be forever known for their "superstrat"-type guitars with pointed headstocks. The Jackson DK2 Dinky is a classic example of this genre. The body is of alder with a flame maple veneer on the transparent colored models and is also available in a range of custom colors and designs. Pickups are by Seymour Duncan (two singlecoils and a humbucker) and the tremolo is Floyd Rose licensed. The rock maple neck has 24 jumbo frets on a compound radius rosewood fingerboard with sharkfin inlays. Jackson is currently owned by Fender and current models such as the DK2 are made in Japan.

Jackson Randy Rhoads

The Randy Rhoads guitar was Jackson Guitars' very first model. It is a sharkfin-shaped guitar somewhat reminiscent of a Flying V but much more pointed. It typically has an alder body and maple neck, although woods vary. Other features include a pointed headstock and sharkfin inlays on the 22-fret ebony fingerboard. The guitar usually has a pair of humbucking pickups and a Floyd Rose tremolo. It was commissioned by Randy Rhoads, the guitarist who played with Ozzy Osbourne and Quiet Riot. Unfortunately, Rhoads was killed in a plane crash before the guitar went into production, having only seen a pair of prototypes before tragedy struck. (see the Mark Morton model pictured below)

Jaydee Supernatural Bass

JayDee Guitars are built in the UK by John Diggins, a one-time employee of the luthier John Birch. The JayDee Supernatural Bass was made famous by Mark King of Level 42. Features include a five-piece laminated neck and body center with Brazilian mahogany outriggers, fully bound neck and headstock, and 21 fret ebony fingerboard inlaid with pearl dot or Saturn/crescent markers. The two pickups have polished hardwood covers, and the bass has an onboard three-band EQ system providing unlimited tone variation. The bass is finished in cherry red or pearl finishes with gold Schaller machine heads and hardware.

Joannes Josephus Derazey, scroll body guitar, 1840

The "scroll guitar", part of the R. Krause collection, is an intriguing gut-string guitar from 1840 and is of quite singular design featuring an unusual scroll feature on the body to either side of the neck. The guitar is attributed to Joannes Josephus Derazey of Paris/Mirecourt. This is almost certainly an alternate spelling of the name Jean Joseph Honoré Derazey, a violin maker who completed his apprenticeship in Mirecourt then worked for several workshops in Paris before joining Jean-Baptist Vuillaume's workshop in around 1840. We know that his production was abundant and that he did indeed build the occasional guitar.

Jerry Jones "Dolphin Nose" Baritone

Jerry Jones Guitars of Nashville, Tennessee, specialize in vintage Danelectro reproductions. Based on the 56 U2 model, the "Dolphin Nose" Baritone uses the same construction of masonite on a wooden frame, but is a better quality build with more attention to detail. As a baritone, it has a 28" scale length and is tuned a 5th or 4th below standard. The "dolphin nose" headstock is of the 6-in-a-line variety based on an old Danelectro design. Pickups are Jerry Jones' own Lipstick Tubes while tuners and adjustable bridge are by Gotoh. It's a perfect baritone for those who love the Danelectro look and sound but want a higher quality instrument.

Kawai Aquarius

Kawai of Japan is better known for their pianos and other keyboard instruments but actually started building guitars in 1964. However, the Aquarius was an original model from the early 1980s. It is made from solid maple and has a 22-fret maple neck and fingerboard. The layout is very Strat-like. The electrics on the Aquarius consist of two humbuckers, a 3-way switch, volume control and tone control with a push/pull pot to allow coil tapping. The guitar is a well-built, comfortable player and with the coil tap facility is very versatile.

Kawai Moonsault

The crescent-shaped Kawai Moonsault is a thing of beauty. Dating from the early 1980s, it was built in Japan for the Japanese market. Despite the obvious shape difference, it has a Les Paul quality to it. The bound body and set-neck are made of mahogany, and the 22-fret bound ebony neck features abalone "phase of the moon" fingerboard inlays. The hardware and humbucking pickups are made by Gotoh, and the electrics are comprised of a master volume, two tones and a three-way switch. Despite a shape that appears impractical, this is a comfortable guitar to play whether seated or standing.

Kay Barney Kessel Pro

Barney Kessel was a jazz guitarist and session player whose career spanned from the early 1940s to his retirement in 1992, and who played with jazz greats such as Oscar Peterson and Sonny Rollins, as well as on pop records by the likes of The Beach Boys and The Monkees. The Kay Barney Kessel Pro (available 1957-1961) is a single cutaway archtop with laminated maple body and spruce top without f-holes and with one or two "Gold K" single coil pickups. It had an elaborate art-deco "Kelvinator" headstock and an acrylic pickguard. Kessel's name was taken off the guitar in 1960 when he started using Gibsons' name instead.

Kay Epitome Lap Steel

The Kay Epitome Lap Steel, circa 1940, has an hourglass-shaped one-piece neck and body. The fingerboard is made from an unknown wood stained to look like ebony and, unusually for a lap steel, is fretted rather than having fret markers. Because of the playing style, lap steels do not require actual frets, just some form of reference. A single coil pickup sits near the bridge on a black metal panel with bakelite volume and tone controls on either side of the strings. The lap steel has a cream-over-gold crinkle finish and would originally have been available with a matching amplifier.

Kay K-45 Travel Guitar (aka The Austin Hatchet)

The Kay K-45 is a full-scale travel guitar with an abbreviated body-shape and compact headstock. Made in Korea, it is of through-neck construction built from mahogany with a maple center section. The neck is thick and rounded like a baseball bat, with a rosewood fingerboard featuring brass inlays. The nut is also brass and the bridge is gold-colored. Pickups are two DiMarzio-designed Super Distortion humbuckers with tone controls for each, master volume and pickup selector and phase toggles. In the USA the guitar, with slightly different specs (e.g. different headstock design), was marketed as the Austin Hatchet. (see picture below)

"So, once I get writing I really try and put five to eight hours a day in my room with a guitar to really try and come up with stuff that feels interesting enough to me to keep it."
- Catie Curtis

Kay Kraft Venetian Model B

In the 1930s Stromberg-Voisenet built guitars for the Kay Musical Instrument Company in Chicago. The elaborately decorated Kay Kraft Model B was available from 1932 to 1937. The unusual asymmetrical body shape can't quite be said to be a cutaway design. It features fancy gold decals on front and back plus a pearloid headstock. A more revolutionary feature is the adjustable neck/body joint which allows the neck to be reset quickly and easily. Also interesting is the double sided bakelite bridge, compensated on one side for Spanish-style playing and straight on other for lap-style.

Michael Kelly Hybrid

The Michael Kelly Hybrid promises screaming electric and sweet acoustic tones in a single guitar. It has an active Fishman piezo pickup in the bridge and a Rockfield SWC humbucker, which are selected using a three-way switch to give either pickup individually or a blend of the two. Each pickup has its own volume control, with the piezo volume doubling as a blend knob when using both sound sources together. Neck and body are built from mahogany, the body being chambered to enhance the acoustic performance. The top is Triple A maple and the guitar has a set neck with rosewood fingerboard and Grover tuners.

Kif Acoustic Bass

Living in West Cornwall, Kif has built boats, fitted kitchens, made replica Art Deco furniture, designed jewelry, bred tropical butterflies and built guitars. In the guitar world, he is known for is his acoustic bass, which was designed specifically to function as a bass. The bolt-on neck has no heel and is made from a minimum of three pre-cut pieces. Bodies tend to be of a laminate construction and use a 2.7mm laminate top. Kif's own-design bracing is lightweight and transfers string energy in a totally unconventional way, allowing for a greater tonal bandwidth while maintaining volume. Kif's unique design makes for a superb sounding individually-styled bass.

Killer KB Simmony Bass

The Killer KB Simmony Bass is a model not often seen outside of Japan, looking like a Rickenbacker 4001 that has been flipped over and crossed with an Ibanez Iceman. It is a replica of the Beelze signature model bass of Toshiya from the Japanese rock band Dir en grey. The bass has a body of alder and a bolt-on maple neck with 23 frets on a rosewood fingerboard. Pickups are Killer's own brand Jazz Bass units and each has its own volume and tone. The headstock is another area where it looks like Rickenbacker was an influence.

Kinkade Acoustic Bass

Kinkade Guitars are completely handmade by Jonny Kinkade in Bristol, UK. The acoustic bass is designed specifically to respond to the frequencies developed by a long scale (34") instrument. The body has a width of 18" at its widest point and is made from mahogany with a Sitka spruce soundboard. The rosewood bridge is positioned in the centers of the vibrating part of the soundboard for tonal efficiency while the internal bracing is designed to give an even response across all the strings. The neck is mahogany with a 21-fret rosewood fingerboard. The bass is available with or without a Florentine cutaway, in fretted or fretless options.

Kinkade Cubist Braque

The Kinkade Cubist Braque guitar is a fully playable piece of art based on one appearing in the painting "Guitar and Bottle of Marc on a Table" by George Braque in 1930. It was chosen because the painting features a good frontal elevation of the guitar. The guitar as realised by Kinkade looks as if it has been lifted right off the canvas. It has a scale length of nearly 19" with a recommended tuning of "G". Beneath the painted acrylic, the guitar is made of mahogany and has a top of Western red cedar.

Klein GK

The Klein GK is a rather odd-looking guitar. Its unusual body shape is reminiscent of the Ovation Breadwinner. However, it was designed with ergonomics in mind. The body is shaped so that the right arm has plenty of support while the lower horn extends downward so that the neck is angled towards the player when seated. The GK also features several Steinberger-like attributes including the headless design, Trans-Trem bridge (a tremolo used to change tunings) and EMG pickups. Despite no longer being in production, it is considered a classic and is often emulated by luthiers specializing in ergonomic guitars. (see picture below and opposite)

Knutsen 11-string Harp Guitar

In 1897 Chris Knutsen was granted a patent for his "one-arm harp guitar" which had a hollow body extension holding 5 to 7 strings. Knutsen was contracted to build guitars for W.J. Dyer & Bro in 1899, but in 1902 Dyer switched to using the Larson Brothers, possibly because their work was consistent whereas no two Knutsen guitars were alike. Knutsens were known for little idiosyncratic features such as fanned frets (pre-Novax!) and rope marquetry binding. Knutsen was also an early advocate of the solid headstock as opposed to the slotted headstock. He was a builder ahead of his time with a taste for experimentation.

Kramer Nightswan

The Kramer Nightswan, a signature model for Vivian Campbell of Def Leppard, started life as the "Shredder" built by Buddy Blaze Guitars of Texas after talks with Campbell. Blaze was hired by Kramer as a business associate and took the "Shredder" guitar with him where it was renamed the Nightswan. It has a mahogany body with deep lower cutaway for higher fret access; two Seymour Duncan humbuckers in the bridge and middle positions with a single volume and three-way-switch; Floyd Rose tremolo; and 24" scale neck with diagonal dot inlays on an ebony fretboard. The guitar is topped off with Schaller tuners on a reverse-angled banana headstock. (see picture on opposite page)

Kramer Ripley Stereo Guitar

The Kramer Ripley Stereo Guitar, designed by Steve Ripley, was introduced to the market in 1985 and promoted by Eddie Van Halen. It is very similar to a Kramer Baretta but features a multi-channel Bartolini humbucker in the bridge position. Each of this pickup's six poles has its own output so that each string can be positioned anywhere in the stereo spectrum using six individual pan knobs on the body. From the guitar the output is fed into a splitter box and then to two amplifiers. To hear the Ripley Stereo guitar in action, listen to "Top Jimmy" on Van Halen's 1984 album.

Kramer XL98 Bass

The XL98 Bass is from Kramer's aluminum neck era from 1976 to 1985, which was a concept inherited from Travis Bean Guitars, with whom Gary Kramer was involved before founding Kramer Guitars. Unlike the Travis Beans, the Kramer necks had their backs inlaid with wood to provide warmth. The XL series itself debuted in 1980. The XL98 Bass is similar to the XL9 Bass but has eight strings arranged in four pairs. The headstock of the bass has four tuners while the four tuners for the octave strings are located at the base of the body in a recess.

Gary Kramer R36 Turbulence

In 2005 Gary Kramer, original founder of Kramer Guitars (now owned by Gibson), started a new company, Gray Kramer Guitars. The R36 Turbulence is an ergonomic Delta-wing design with unhindered access to its 36-fret neck. The fretboard is so long that there is only room for a single humbucker between it and the tremolo bridge. It also comes with two different fret sizes - jumbo frets from 1-24 and skinny tall frets from 25-36 - so as to achieve better fret spacing at the top of the neck. The R36 Turbulence is a seven-string guitar ranging sonically from a low B to the fourth octave on the high E.

LaBaye 2x4

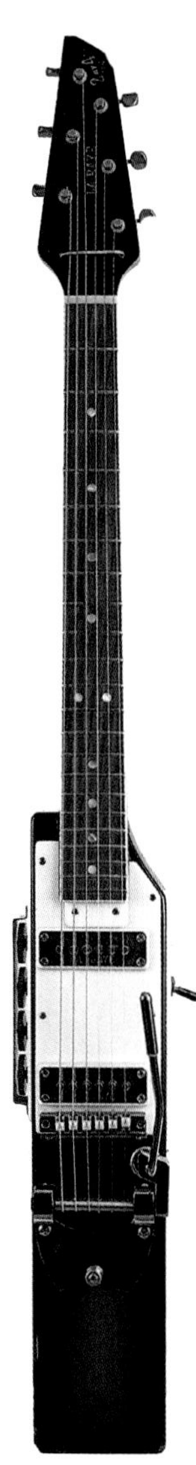

The LaBaye 2x4 entered production in the Holman-Woodell factory in Neodesha, Kansas, in 1967. The guitar resembles a 2-by-4 plank with a neck stuck on it, hence the name. Neck, pickups and vibrato are identical to those appearing on other brand guitars built at the same factory. Controls are positioned on the top edge of the guitar except for the pickup selector, which is on the bottom edge. Bass and 12-string versions were also made, but none were successful and production ceased within a year. The only notable player is Devo's Bob Mothersbaugh who uses a LaBaye live on the solo to "Mr DNA". (see picture right)

Lace Helix Maya Series HG-01

Lace is probably best known for its pickups but has its own range of guitars, too. The Lace Helix series is particularly futuristic in appearance having a 3-D swept-shaped body constructed using two-piece alder. The fretboard is 12" radius ebony with a graphite nut with 22 jumbo frets on a set maple neck. Hardware is chrome including Grover Chrome Mini-Rotomatic tuners and the bridge and volume knob. But the main attractions here are two Alumitone singlecoil pickups and Alumitone humbucker Low-Boy-style split coil pickup, giving more bass, more volume, clear smooth highs and increased resonance.

Lacote 7-string, 1820

The concept of guitars with more strings than is usual is not a new phenomenon. The first 6-string guitars were merely Baroque 5-string guitars with an additional bass string. Some 19th Century guitars, however, had floating strings. The Lacote 7-string guitar from 1820 in the Musee de la Musique, Paris, for example, has a seventh string running parallel to the others but off the fretboard. The headstock has an extension to accommodate it. This extra string would have usually been tuned to a drop D or occasionally C. A similar guitar exists in the private collection of Bernhard Kresse. (see picture on opposite page)

Lacote Curulli Decacorde

The Musee de la Musique in Paris has two Lacote Decacordes from 1826 and 1830 in its collection. The Decacorde, as its name suggests, is a 10-string guitar with five fretted strings and five floating basses. Built by French guitar maker René Lacote, these guitars were very possibly played by Ferdinando Carulli himself. Carulli (1770-1841), one of the most eminent composers for classical guitar, was known to have worked with Lacote with a view to improving the guitar and would definitely have experimented with concepts such as extra strings.

Laguna LG4CE BUB

The LG4BUB acoustic, from California's Laguna Guitars, has a luxuriant acoustic tone with the playability of an electric. It features a grand-orchestra body style with Florentine cutaway, darkened Bubinga top, back and sides, mahogany neck, bound body and fingerboard with offset dot markers. It is fitted with a Fishman "Classic 4 T" preamp with tuner. A transparent red quilted ash version is also available.

Yuri Landman Moonlander

The Moonlander was built by Yuri Landman for Lee Ronaldo of Sonic Youth. The most unusual feature of the Moonlander is that it has a second headstock bolted on top of the first one. From here, a set of 12 drone strings stretch down to a bridge on the bass side of the body. Landman describes the Moonlander as having a sound "almost like you are playing in a cathedral" and is keen to point out that it is not a harp guitar but a sympathetic string guitar. He has also experimented in having the six strings on the neck arranged in two courses of three strings.

Langcaster

Joh Lang of New Zealand's Langcaster Guitars builds the most beautiful Strat-type guitars out of Kauri, which at 35,000 years old is the oldest wood ever used in the construction of a guitar. Kauri (Agatha Australis) only grows on the North Island of New Zealand, and is sometimes referred to as the dinosaur of the flora. Petrified kauri has been found in the swamps of Northern New Zealand, preserved for over 30,000 years; this is the wood that Joh Lang uses for his guitar bodies.

Lapstick

The Lapstick must be the world's smallest travel guitar. With a minimal body and headless design, this short scale guitar is compact enough to fit into an overcoat pocket. Built from mahogany with a rosewood fretboard, the Lapstick has a 17.9" scale and an overall length of 19.9". It has a single EMG Select pickup and an onboard pre-amp allowing it to be played anywhere while using earphones. Because of its short scale an A tuning is recommended, although with heavier strings it can be tuned to G.

Christophe LeDuc Utopia Bass

The LeDuc Utopia - or U-Bass - built by Christophe LeDuc, is a modern-day interpretation of the semi-acoustic bass. The bass features a "free floating" sound table of spruce mounted onto a body of ash. The sound table, working with the bridge, acts as a percussive top and translates the nuances of play, limiting buzzes and increasing the sustain. LeDuc also builds a fretless version of the U-Bass with a mahogany body and a sound table of red cedar which optimizes the low medium frequencies of the instrument.

Simon Lee Cyclotron Guitars "Jasper"

Simon Lee trained as a guitar maker at Merton College, Oxford, but was unhappy about using tropical hardwoods and set about designing an environmentally friendly guitar. Cyclotron guitars are built in a sandwich design using recycled plastics from a variety of sources including off-cuts from industrial pipes, vending machine coffee cups, plastic bottles, crushed CDs and yoghurt pots. The Jasper guitar nicely shows off the sandwich design, which has a tiered effect and consists of a sustainable maple core supporting the maple neck (also sustainable), pickups and bridge with the front and back panels of recycled material bolted into place.

Lehua Plexiglass Lap Steel

Lehua lap steel guitars are not a well-known brand. A particularly rare example is made of colored lucite over a timber frame, dating possibly from the late 1940s to early 50s. The top of the instrument is blue lucite with a clear lucite raised fingerboard adorned with multi-colored position markers on its underside. The pickup cover is also blue, while bridge, tailpiece, nut, tuning buttons and control knobs are all made of clear perspex with red detailing. If that was not enough, the whole guitar lights up thanks to two 110v bulbs positioned underneath the fingerboard.

Levinson Blade RH4

Levinson Blade, sounding like a 1920s private eye from detective fiction, is the name given to a series of guitars originally built in Switzerland by Gary Levinson. Levinson approached building guitars from an analytical standpoint, being deeply interested in the inherent resonance frequencies of wood and tonal effects of hardware. The RH4 is the original Blade guitar. Visually it looks very much like a Strat, but is a meticulously designed and assembled Strat with a body of Sen ash, hard rock maple neck, ebony fingerboard, gold hardware, Sperzel tuners, Falcon tremolo and onboard treble/bass boost and mid boost for the two V-3 stacked coils and LH-55 Vintage humbucker.

VOLUME
TONE
TONE

Eduard Lieves, Doublecut Guitar, 1810

The guitar built by Eduard Lieves from Königsberg, Germany, (now Kaliningrad, Russia), circa 1810, is an interesting example of 19th Century guitar building, and displays an early occurrence of the double cutaway body design. This body style is commonly associated with modern electric guitars but this guitar proves that the concept had been around for a lot longer. The top appears to be spruce and is inlaid either side of the ebony bridge with an intricate vine design. The back of the guitar is quite stunning and features what appears to be book-matched quilted maple. The guitar is from the collection of R. Krause.

Lindert Locomotive T

Lindert Guitars were produced in Chelan Falls, in Wenatchee, Washington, from 1986. Unfortunately, the company ceased trading in 2002 even after having moved production to Korea. The Lindert Locomotive T (most models had railway-inspired names) is a Tele-shaped guitar with enough original features to prevent it from being a mere copy. The body is made from molded resin and features a cut-out design with inserts of tweed around the bridge resembling the speaker on a vintage radio. The neck has an "escape velocity" profile - half rounded, half V-shaped - for faster playing action, and is topped off with Lindert's trademark "thumbs up" headstock. (see picture opposite)

> *"The most important part of my religion is to play guitar."* - Lou Reed

Liquid Metal Guitars LMG GGG #001

Liquid Metal Guitars of Vancouver was founded by Phil Cook who, inspired by TV shows such as American Chopper, Biker Build Off and OverHaulin', in which teams build amazing bikes or cars, decided he wanted to do the same thing with guitars built from metal. One of their first creations, the model GGG #001, is an 18K gold plated metal-bodied guitar. It is a flat-topped semi-hollow guitar built from aluminium alloy, with two humbuckers, volume and tone control knobs, three-way pickup selector and wrap-around intoned bridge, all finished flawlessly in gold. The sustain is said to be amazing.

Little Guitar Works Torzal Standard Bass

Jerome Little of Little Guitar Works in Austin, Texas, specializes in building basses with a Torzal natural twist which offers a more natural and efficient interaction with the human body and reduces the risk of repetitive strain injuries such as carpal tunnel syndrome and tendonitis. The neck of the bass is twisted, placing each of the player's hands in a more natural position at either end of the instrument. The twist is 15 degrees towards the player at the bridge, and 20 degrees rotating away from the player at the nut, giving a total rotation of 35 degrees. (see picture opposite)

Lone Star LSSG 6 Pedal Steel

The LSSG 6 Lite is a compact, lightweight pedal steel with maple top and front and back skirts. It is a six-string with a recommended drop E tuning. The three pedals and four knee levers are used to accommodate the most popular pitch changes, and it can also be set up for A6 or C6 tunings. Two Fender Texas Special pickups are mounted on a moving bracket to allow tone changes by altering the position of the unit. With a length of 30", weight of 17lbs, and a scale length of 24", by pedal steel standards this is a travel guitar!

LongBow American Classic 2-String Bass

The Longbow American Classic 2-String Bass is delightfully simple, resembling a long block of wood with pickups, tuners and two bass strings attached. Which is basically what it is. It is fretless and available in short, medium, long or extra-long scales, with pickups placed in regular or "EB" positions (the latter supposedly being good for dub reggae). It is made from one piece of American hard maple, with tung oil natural finish, two magnetic humbucking single string pickups and ABM single string adjustable chrome bridges. The strings are tuned to E and A, and it is said to have fantastic sustain.

Augustino Loprinzi

Augustino LoPrinzi Guitars of Florida make very exacting hand-crafted nylon and steel-strung acoustic guitars to the highest specifications. The father and daughter team of Augustino and Donna LoPrinzi approach instrument building as a blending of luthier skills, knowledge and art. The use of high quality seasoned woods is essential to LoPrinzi. The absolute minimum age of wood used in an instrument is two years, with the age going up to that of their stash of Brazilian rosewood purchased in 1963. The Nova Futura classical guitar, with soundports to either side of the neck, has excellent tone, great sustain and unprecedented power.

Lowernherz 00907 4-string Bass (12 pickups)

Löwenherz Basses are custom made in Germany. The design incorporates an upper cutaway resembling an ocean wave, a lower cutaway resembling a lobster's claw, and a hefty brass lion's head which acts as the tailpiece and which increases the incredible sustain of these basses. Each bass has no less than six pickups, which can be used in any combination, giving a diverse range of tones. However, one particular custom order, #00907, has what appears to be one huge pickup that is actually 12 individual pickups in a single casing, with two rows of six on-off switches for each of the pickups. (see picture opposite)

Leonardo Lospennato Nuax X-Dream

Leonardo Lospennato Concept Basses and Guitars are handmade in Berlin, Germany. The X-Dream guitar is a stylish design that is at once futuristic and retro. The design seems to combine elements from both the Gibson Firebird and Fernandes Vertigo. The mahogany body has a bolt-on flamed maple neck with a 24.75" scale. The fingerboard is available in a choice of timbers and has 24 stainless steel frets and mother of pearl dot position markers. Pickups are two Seymour Duncans, and other hardware includes Gotoh 510 tuners, Earvana compensated nut and a tri-dimensionally adjustable Schaller 3DP bridge.

Lucida Guitarron

Lucida Guitars builds distinguished lines of classical and flamenco guitars alongside traditional mariachi instruments. The Guitarron is a six-string acoustic bass used in mariarchi bands. It has a huge, rounded body, and is known for its booming bass tone. It is built from natowood with a rosewood fretless fingerboard and decorative wood body binding. Other features are a spruce bridge, inlaid soundhole rosette, herringbone purfling and elephant ear tuners. It also features authentic nylon strings from Mexico. By modern bass standards it has a very short scale at 26". It is not an instrument known for its sustain qualities but rather for its seriously fat tone.

Luna Henna Oasis

Yvonne de Villiers founded Luna Guitars inspired by her mother Hilda Williers, a professional bass player for over 40 years who often struggled with awkwardly-shaped, heavy instruments. Luna Guitars were created to be ergonomic, lighter weight instruments designed to fit the bodies of those of a smaller stature. The Henna Oasis is a 25" scale steel-string acoustic with mahogany neck, maple back and sides and top of spruce or solid cedar. The top, back and headstock feature a laser-etched design by Henna artist Alex Morgan. The guitar has a built-in Orion pre-amp/tuner and is just under 15" at its widest point. (see picture opposite)

Luna Andromeda Dragon Bass

The Andromeda Dragon Bass has a full 34” scale on a featherweight sculpted basswood body with an extended top horn so that it balances well on a strap. The neck is made of maple with a rosewood 24-fret fingerboard inlaid with mother of pearl moon phase fret markers. Pickups are active J and MM style and the bridge is composed of four Monolithic individual string units. The bass is finished in Raven Gloss (i.e. black) and features an abalone dragon inlay on the top half of the body. The whole instrument weighs just 7lbs. (see the Andromeda opposite, and the Paz Signature Bass below)

LUNA

Maccaferri Plastic Guitar

Selmer Maccaferri Gypsy Jazz guitars, favored by Django Reinhardt, were invented by Mario Maccaferri. Maccaferri had a later career in the production of plastic consumer goods. In 1948 he combined his interests and produced the Islander plastic ukulele, the first plastic stringed instrument. In 1953 he introduced plastic guitars, which were intended as serious highly-functional instruments. These included a round-hole Islander guitar, and a Gypsy Jazz guitar with cutaway and f-holes. In the early 1980s, a stockpile of these guitars was discovered in a warehouse in brand new condition, and suddenly they were everywhere. Dave Stewart of the Eurythmics bought one and used it on TV appearances. (see picture left)

Magnatone Amerloha Lap Steel

The Magnatone Amerloha Lap Steel is a very basic-looking instrument, and indeed is quite simple. But what it lacks in complexity it more than makes up for in decoration. The one-piece body, a diminutive traditional guitar-shaped affair, is completely covered in a pearloid or "Mother of Toilet Seat" finish. Such finishes came in a range of colors including blue, green, grey and plum. The printed fingerboard has a stepped cutaway effect to the bass side as it approaches the higher frets. The pickup is concealed in the body underneath the pearloid and is covered by a handrest over the strings.

Peter Malinoski Art Guitars

Peter Malinoski is an artist and maker of one-off guitars and basses which he calls "art guitars" as they are often of a very visual nature and would be quite at home in an art gallery. Bodies have a very rounded organic feel to them, and headstocks too are usually rounded with the tuners arranged in an arc. Wooden pickguards are oval-shaped and may contain hidden pickups. However, form over function is unlikely to be the case with these guitars because they all appear to be perfectly playable instruments and the rounded flowing shapes should be quite comfortable too.

Malden Movak

Malden Guitars are based in California and manufactured in Korea. Their Movak model has a very familiar appearance with a body shaped like a Fender Jazzmaster but with the pickups, bridge and electrics of a Telecaster. Perfect for the Jazzmaster fan who wants a Tele sound. The body is made of alder or basswood, and the bolt-on maple neck has a rosewood fingerboard with 21 narrow and tall frets and dot inlays.

Malden Subhuman

The Subhuman from Malden Guitars is an original design, looking something like an edgier, more metal version of the Parker Fly. The body is made of mahogany and has a set-in mahogany neck with rosewood fingerboard and 22 medium jumbo frets. It is of hardtail design with strings loaded through the body and has two Tesla VR-Extreme humbuckers with one volume, one tone (with coil-tap) and a three-way switch. The finish is black with binding on the body, neck and headstock, and the hardware is nickel-plated. (see another member of the Malden family below)

Malmberg Abba Star Guitar

The Star Guitar played by Abba's Björn Ulvaeus for their 1974 Eurovision Song Contest-winning entry "Waterloo", was designed and built by Goram Malmberg. In Malmberg's own words: "The guitar had to serve a practical purpose therefore the horns point in logical directions, and the strap has to be fastened in a good balance position. There should be no horn where one has the right arm. There has to be a horn to place the volume and tone knobs. So the design issue was to find a design balance that included those features. The body is laminate plywood, for the reason that the edge of the horns should not break. It is all solid as a Strat with good sustain. The paint was in fact a Hot Rod car flake on a silver base with 100 layers of varnish on top." The original guitar was lost long ago, but Malmberg has created a replica for Stockholm's Abba museum.

Andy Manson Mermaid

The Mermaid is a fully functional and playable musical sculpture taking the form of a beautifully carved life-size mermaid with tumbling hair, naked torso and scaled, curved tail. She is also a beautiful sounding acoustic guitar, but perhaps is not of the most convenient shape for extended performances. She was handcrafted over the course of three years by Andy Manson of Devon, UK, and took three years to build. Manson has built instruments for Jimmy Page, John Paul Jones, Ian Anderson, Martin Barre, Andy Summers, and Mike Oldfield.

Manson MB-1 Matt Bellamy Signature

The Manson MB-1 Matt Bellamy Signature guitar is based on the Muse frontman's first Hugh Manson-built guitar and is constructed with an alder body, birds eye maple neck and rosewood fingerboard. It is fitted with an MBK humbucker at the bridge, a Fernandes Sustainer at the neck, volume, tone, kill switch and Sustainer switches. However, the guitar has a unique feature in the shape of a MIDI control screen mounted behind the bridge, which is used to send digital information from the guitar to control digital effects units.

"I don't play a lot of fancy guitar. I don't want to play it. The kind of guitar I want to play is mean, mean licks."
- John Lee Hooker

C.F. Martin & Co.
EST. 1833

Martin 000-28LDB Lonnie Donegan Signature Edition

The "King of Skiffle", Lonnie Donegan had over twenty Top 30 hits in the UK between 1955 and 1962, and was honored with a Martin Signature guitar in 2002. The 000-28LDB has back, sides, and headstock overlay of Brazilian rosewood. The top is Sitka spruce with hand-scalloped 5/16" X-bracing for a rich, balanced tone. The low profile neck is carved from solid mahogany and both fingerboard and bridge are black African ebony. For optimum tone, the nut and compensated saddle are made from bone. The guitar finished is 1935-style sunburst, with soundhole rosette inlaid with paua shell, and fingerboard inlays spelling out "SKIFFLE", and Donegan's name between the 18th and 20th frets.

Martin 018T Tenor Guitar

Martin made tenor guitars from 1927. The 0-size tenor guitar is actually of a smaller size than the 0-size 6-string. The 0-18T was first made in 1929 and was in production until the early 2000s. It was popularized in the 1960s by Nick Reynolds of the Kingston Trio. With a 23" scale, lower bout measurement of 13" and a 13/16" wide nut, the guitar has mahogany back and sides, spruce top, 20 fret Brazilian rosewood fingerboard with pearl dot inlays, and Brazilian rosewood for the bridge and headstock overlay. Other features include tortoiseshell plastic pickguard and body binding, and individual open gear tuners.

"Steve Vai joined my dad's band right around the time when I actually started playing guitar. So he gave me a couple of lessons on fundamentals, and gave me some scales and practice things to work on. But I pretty much learned everything by ear." - Dweezil Zappa

Martin 1830s scroll-head Stauffer Guitar

The Martin "scroll-head" Stauffer guitar dates from 1830. C.F. Martin served as an apprentice to J.A. Stauffer of Vienna, a highly respected 19th Century luthier, and most of Martin's early guitars up until around 1840 were based on Stauffer's designs. A couple of idiosyncratic features of these were a neck that was adjustable using a clock key in the heel, and the "scroll" or "Persian slipper" headstock shape with 6-in-a-line tuners, which was later popularized by the Fender Telecaster and electric guitars ever since.

Martin D-35 Johnny Cash Acoustic

A beautifully designed homage to Mr. Cash with grained ivoroid binding and heelcap, star-shaped fretboard inlays and Johnny's signature in mother of pearl inlaid between the 19th and 20th frets on the fingerboard. However, this guitar isn't just about the looks; unlike Martin's D-35 and HD-35, this was lovingly crafted out of Engelmann instead of Sitka spruce, which means the sound is as silky as the finish, and can fill a room without the need for electrical help. (see picture below)

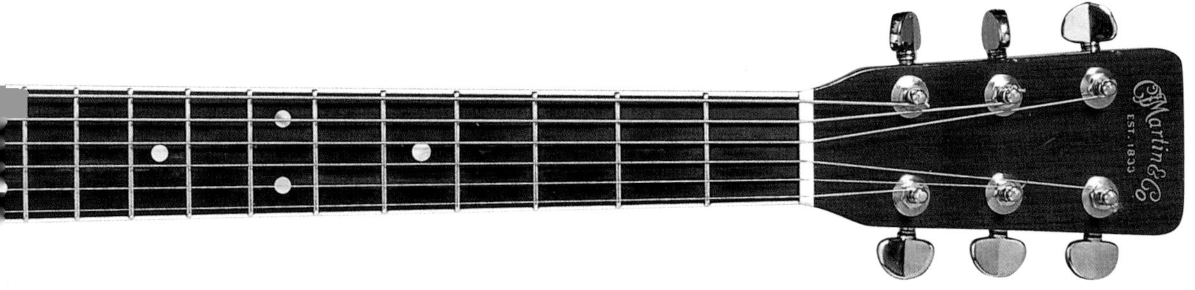

Martin F-65 Electric Guitar

Although Martin is known for its acoustic guitars, they have dabbled with electrics. The F-65, in production between 1962 and 1965, is a hollowbody electric with a double cutaway tulip-bud body shape. The guitar is fitted with a pair of DeArmond pickups, each with its own volume and tone controls, a three-way switch and a Bigsby-like "M" vibrato. The body has binding on both sides, with back, sides and archtop being constructed of maple plywood, the top featuring two ornately-shaped f-holes. The neck is unbound mahogany with a Brazilian rosewood fingerboard, and with - rather incongruous on an electric - the familiar square Martin headstock.

Martin SWOMGT

The Martin SWOMGT is a sustainable series special edition constructed with solid cherry sides, back and neck, solid spruce top and katalox (Mexican hardwood) fretboard and bridge. The cherry and katalox timbers are sourced from forests managed in a sustainable and ecologically responsible manner, while the spruce top and internal bracing are from reclaimed pulp logs. The guitar features a 000 style body with low profile OM neck, and a 25.4" scale. Headstock veneer, body binding, backstrip, heelcap, endpiece and pickguard are all tortoiseshell plastic.

Maton MS500/HC

Founded in 1946 by Bill May, the Maton Musical Instruments Company, based in Melbourne, is Australia's longest running and most successful guitar manufacturer. They pioneered the use of many Australian wood species in guitar construction. The MS500 Mastersound guitar, inspired by the increasing popularity of rock and roll, was launched in 1958. It has a body of silver silkwood, and a 12" radius bolt-on Queensland maple neck with rosewood fingerboard inlaid with pearl dots. Two humbuckers are controlled via master volume and tone knobs, with a coil tap for the bridge pickup, and a 3-way rotary selector switch.

Maton Starline

The Starline is a singlecut hollowbodied archtop electric. It was originally produced in the 1940s when it was Maton's flagship model. The Starline 4606 is the 60th Anniversary model and has a body and set neck of Queensland maple. The carved top is of Sitka spruce and the fingerboard is ebony with mother of pearl block inlays. The guitar features two humbuckers with a volume and tone control for each, plus master volume (with coil tap) and 3-way selector switch. The guitar is finished in an immaculate gloss Tri-Burst. Bridge, tailpiece and Grover tuners are all gold-plated.

Maverick X1

Built in Korea and assembled in the UK, the Maverick X1 is an obviously metal-flavored design reminiscent of the BC Rich Mockingbird, with a longer lower horn and an extended upper bout offering right arm support. This design gives the guitar perfect balance when played in any position. The body is basswood and the neck is made of maple with a bubinga 24-fret fingerboard, topped off with an upside down 6-in-a-line headstock. Two humbuckers are controlled via a 3-way switch and roller-style volume and tone pots set into carved recesses at the lower edge of the guitar.

Brian May Red Special

Queen guitarist Brian May built his unique sounding Red Special when he was 16, aided by his father. Most of the wood used was from an 18th century fireplace mantel. The neck is thick, flat and wide with a 24-fret oak fingerboard inlaid with position markers hand-shaped from pearl buttons and lacquered with Rustin's Plastic Coating. The tremolo uses motorcycle valve springs and has an arm made from a bicycle's saddle bag carrier with the tip fashioned from a knitting needle. May also rewound three Burns Tri-Sonic pickups to use in the guitar. Many replicas have been built, with officially-licensed copies produced by Guild, Burns, and, more recently, Brian May's own BM Guitars. (see picture right)

David Thomas McNaught Phoenix Rising

McNaught Guitars, based in North Carolina, are hand-crafted by David McNaught and finished by Dave Mansel. The Phoenix Rising is an original design double cutaway guitar featuring a clear-finished Honduran mahogany set-through neck, known for its transfer of tone and added sustain. The body is of clear-finished Honduran mahogany, with a carved mahogany top or, optionally,s stunning-looking diamond quilt or flamed maple tops. Fingerboard options include rock maple, Indian rosewood or ebony, all of which are bound in flamed maple binding for a subtle yet classy touch. Scale length, hardware, number of frets, pickups, electronics, etc, are all subject to the customer's specifications.

Meazzi Hollywood Jupiter

The first thing you will notice about the Meazzi Hollywood Jupiter from 1960s Italy is the large chromed metal plates and switches which seem to cover the guitar. Two large sliders are used to mix the neck and bridge pickups and to set neck pickup volume. The bridge pickup is active, powered by a 9-volt battery under the Meazzi logo plate, and creates a cutting ultra-treble. The most unusual feature, however, is a mercury switch which mutes the guitar when it is in an upright position, which means the guitarist could lean the guitar against the amp between sets without having to adjust the amp's volume. It is hardly essential, but is clever nonetheless.

Melobar Sidewinder

The Melobar Sidewinder is a stand-up steel guitar - that is, like a lap steel but played standing, giving the player the freedom to move about the stage. The Melobar stand-up steel was designed by Walt Smith and was built by Semie Moseley of Mosrite Guitars in the mid 1960s. Visually these guitars resemble standard Mosrite electric guitars but with the neck and center section of body tilted up towards the player. Pickups selector switch, volume and tone controls and output jack are located on the downward facing side of the raised center section. The Sidewinder is the name given to the latest generation of Melobar stand-up steels.

Mercurio Carvetop S

The Mercurio Carvetop S is a custom-built boutique-quality guitar featuring a Strat-shaped body of mahogany with a carved maple top and a neck of mahogany with a 22-fret rosewood fingerboard. Where the Mercurio comes into its own, however, is that the guitarist is able to change pickups on the fly. The three pickups are each rear-mounted through panels in the back of the body and are all easily interchangeable with others mounted on the required modules.

Messenger Panther

The Messenger Panther guitar, as played by Mark Farner of Grand Funk Railroad, was manufactured from 1967 to 1968 in Astoria, Oregon. The guitar features an alloy neck that extends into the body and terminates with an internal tuning fork which resonates with the guitar. Some models had a built-in "Tone Messer" fuzz circuit, while a stereo model had separate outputs for both pickups. The guitar is of hollowbodied construction with two cats eye soundholes and non-cutaway design. The alloy neck construction allows it to join the body at the 22nd fret, giving full access to the whole fretboard.

Micro-Frets Golden Melody

Micro-Frets Inc was founded in the 1960s by Ralph Jones who came from an engineering background and who made several innovations that were years ahead of their time. For example, the "Micro-nut" allowed for perfect intonation at both ends of the strings (decades before Buzz Feiten's tuning system and the Earvana nut) and the "Calibrato" vibrato allowed strings to stay in tune (relatively) while the pitch is altered. The Golden Melody, one of the original range of guitars, features a double cutaway asymmetrical body design, semi-hollow body construction, Micro-nut technology, sculpted pickguard, Grover tuners and Calibrato tremolo.

Minarik Inferno 4-String Bass

Arguably one of the strangest shapes for a bass; puns about face melting solos and scorching riffs abound. Minarik claims that the shape was not chosen purely for aesthetic reasons; their theory is that a guitar needs more mass on the side with the bass strings, and 'tone pockets' boost specific frequencies giving the bass a denser sound. At 53.5" from headstock to tail, the shape is not the only thing that will need getting used to. This bass is not for wallflowers; no wonder it was endorsed by Lemmy Kilmister and Gene Simmons.

MiniStar Acoustar

MiniStar Guitars builds a series of travel guitars, and while their electric guitars and basses are extremely minimalistic in design, the Acoustar acoustic guitar does not look out of the ordinary. It features a cutaway body, 25" scale, piezo pickup with 3-band EQ/tuner, and rosewood fingerboard. The back of the body is molded but the big secret is the detachable neck, which means that the whole guitar fits into a small carrying bag. The neck can be re-attached quickly and easily.

"I'm not the kind of guy who deserves to play a vintage guitar because I'm too rough on instruments."
- Tommy Shaw

MiniStar Basstar 5F

The Basstar 5F looks like a very long bass neck with a pickup at the bottom. Designed for portability, the Basstar doesn't have a body as such. It is made of maple and has a J-type pickup with volume and tone knobs on its upper edge. To allow it to balance on a strap or to sit upon your knee it has a selection of metal rods that can be attached to simulate various parts of the instrument's body. It also has attachments that allow it to be played in a stand-up position. The Basstar 5F model is a 5-string fretless and is said to have great sustain despite the lack of any body mass.

Mobius Megatar

The Mobius Megatar is a touch-style guitar. The instrument has 12 strings divided into a set of six bass strings and a set of six melody strings. The fingers of both hands are used to tap or touch the strings against the frets, allowing two parts to be played simultaneously. One hand might play a bass line while the other fingers chords or a melody. One of the top-of-the-line instruments is called 'The Hammer of Thor'. It has dual Bartolini pickups with onboard active circuit plus piezo pickups and a complete MIDI implementation allowing access of synth sounds. It also has optional Novax fanned frets. These instruments have a lot of potential but are not for the faint-hearted. (see picture below)

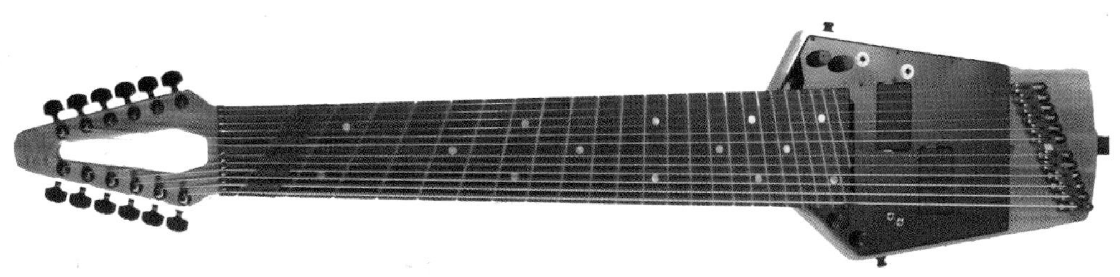

Modulus Graphite Flight 6

The Modulus Graphite Flight 6 Monologue guitar, from 1983, is a small-bodied headless guitar very much in the Steinberger mold. It is constructed out of carbon graphite and so is very nearly indestructible but at the same time very light in weight. It has a much more curved body shape than the near rectangular Steinberger, and also has a hardtail bridge and conventional tuners mounted at the base of the body. However, that shape and those tuners might make it difficult to stand up when not being played. (see picture below)

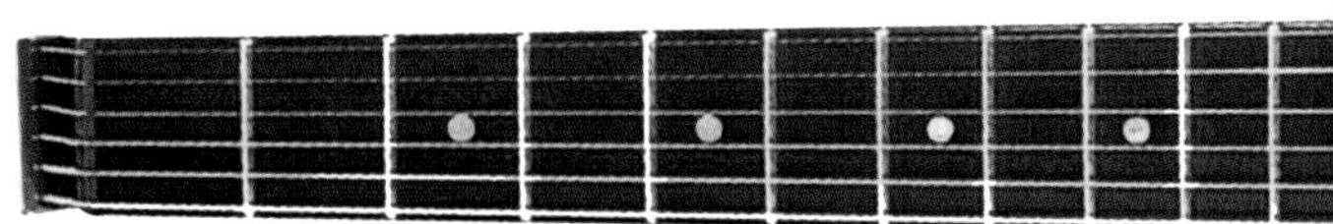

Modulus Quantum Q6 6-string Bass

The Modulus Quantum boasts a massive sustain, earth-shattering low end and versatile tone controls. Standard features include an alder body with a maple top from sustainable sources, and EMG-DC pickups with active bass and treble. The 6-string bass has a neck width of 2" at the nut widening to 3.25" at the 24th fret with the scale length being extra long at 35". It's the neck that Modulus basses are most famous for, and this one is made of aerospace-grade carbon fibre for consistent performance, durability and sustain. (see picture below)

"The guitar was my weapon, my shield to hide behind."
- Brian May

Monson Guitars Baphomet Bass

Brent Monson founded Monson Guitars, currently based in California, in 2001. Inspired by the guitars used by The Misfits, Monson has created a whole portfolio of designs which are a “combination of function and bad ass looks”. The six-stringed fretless Baphomet Bass is a mighty, if scary looking, beast. The pointed, barbed shape isn’t the easiest to describe so I will just say that if the Grim Reaper were to put down his scythe and take up the bass guitar, this is the bass you would expect him to play. (see picture below)

Moog Guitar Paul Vo Collector's Edition

The Moog Guitar Paul Vo Collector's Edition, despite its pedigree, is not a guitar synth and is not a MIDI-guitar. However, it does feature some cool electronics that directly affect the strings of the guitar. With three playing modes - Sustain, Mute and Controlled Sustain - this is a serious yet expensive challenger to Fernandes Sustainer guitars. 'Sustain' gives infinite sustain on every string and at every fret position, 'Mute' is designed for staccato playing as it removes energy from the strings (a sustainer in reverse), and 'Controlled Sustain' sustains the notes being played while muting those that aren't (which the Fernandes system does not do).

Neal Moser Siren

Neal Moser has been working with guitars since 1964 and famously designed the Bich guitar for BC Rich. The Moser Custom Shop, based in California, offers a range of body shapes which can be custom made as neck-through or bolt-on instruments. The Siren model could be said to be a more intricately carved take on the Bich design, with fluid curving lines and multiple points and cutaways. A custom through-neck model could have, for example, a two piece maple neck with mahogany body wings and Macassar ebony fingerboard with antique ivoroid binding, Floyd Rose tremolo and custom electronics.

Neal Moser Spawn SV

The Spawn SV from the Moser Custom Shop is another design which can be custom made as a neck-through or bolt-on neck guitar, and can be highly individualized to the customer's specifications. The body shape is spiky but at the same time graceful and flowing. A typical through-neck would feature elements such as a two-piece laminated mahogany neck-through with mahogany wings and Macassar ebony fingerboard with custom inlay; Grover Rotomatic mini machine head; Kahler Hybrid tremolo; and DiMarzio humbuckers.

Mosrite Brass Rail

The Brass Rail is possibly the rarest of Mosrite's production run instruments (as opposed to one-offs) with only 100 being built. Designed and built by Semie Moseley in 1976 in an attempt to crack the Japanese market, the design features a brass rod deep in the center of the neck with the frets driven directly into it. This apparently produced, as Moseley said, "Sustain like you never heard!" Examples were built with both bolt-on and set necks, with the necks on set-necked models continuing inside the bodies, beneath the pickups, and up to the bridge.

Mosrite Joe Maphis Doubleneck

Joe Maphis, The King of the Strings, was a virtuoso country music guitarist popular in the 1950s and 1960s. His trade mark guitar was a doublenecked Mosrite. His own guitar had two six-string necks with the top one being a shorter-scale octave neck and with his name inlaid into the fingerboards of the two necks. The Joe Maphis production model often combined a 12-string and 6-string neck. It has small low frets, four pickups, volume, tone, 3-way switch and neck selector switch and a Mosrite vibrato on the 6-string. The serial number is stamped into the rosewood itself between the 19th and 20th frets of both necks.

Mosrite Johnny Ramone

The Mosrite Johnny Ramone model is based on the Ventures model II. Johnny bought his original Mosrite Ventures model II in January 1974 for $54 at Manny's Guitar Emporium in New York City. It has a slab body without the German carve that many Mosrite models featured. The Johnny Ramone Signature edition is a replica built in Japan and assembled in the USA. It has a basswood body, maple neck and rosewood fingerboard. Hardware includes Mosrite roller bridge, Grover tuners, DiMarzio singlecoil pickup in the bridge position and Seymour Duncan mini-humbucker in the neck position.

MusicMan Albert Lee

The MusicMan Albert Lee Signature model features the familiar Strat-style three singlecoil pickup layout, but also has a patented 'Silent Circuit' which reduces the hum often associated with this set-up while retaining a true singlecoil sound. The guitar itself has an offset-shaped body of Southern Ash with angular horns. The neck and fingerboard are maple with a 10" radius and 22 frets. The headstock is of the distinctive MusicMan 4+2 design and is only 5-7/8" in length. The neck is perfectly aligned to the body using five bolts, and has a sculpted neck joint allowing smooth access to the higher frets.

MusicMan StingRay Bass

MusicMan, founded in 1971 by ex-Fender employees Forrest White and Tom Walker, initially produced a hybrid tube/solid state amplifier, but with Leo Fender installed as president they began producing instruments in 1976. The StingRay Bass, looking like a sleeker version of the Fender Precision, had a few innovations of its own such as a humbucking pickup and active pre-amp. A 3-band EQ made it possible to boost the mid-range frequencies in addition to the lows and highs, while piezo pickups in the bridge as an optional extra allowed further tone possibilities. The 3+1 layout of the tuners on the headstock has become a highly-recognizable MusicMan trademark.

MusicVox Space Ranger

MusicVox guitars were originally available in 1997 and were designed with an appreciation for vintage guitars with superior tone and iconic aesthetics firmly in mind. The Space Ranger was the first MusicVox model to be unveiled. It has a mahogany body, maple neck and fingerboard and is fitted with a pair of P90, PAF-style or mini-humbucker pickups. While the guitar press raved about the Space Ranger, not everyone was convinced. With features such as the hugely exaggerated lower horn and the large kidney-shaped headstock, some saw it as a visual joke, which is a shame as the eccentric aesthetics actually contributed to the tonal characteristics of the guitar.

National Regal Conservatory

The National Regal Conservatory probably dates from 1936-37 when Regal built guitars for National in Chicago. It is a square-necked lap steel guitar of one-piece cast aluminum construction. It has a black pressed-fiber fingerboard with silver fret lines and understated dot position markers. The casting is quite simple with the edges of the body being flat. On the reverse side, the hollows at the back of the neck and body center are covered with suede-finished plywood panels. The twin-bladed pickup has volume and tone controls, one to each side, with the guitar lead being directly wired into the electrics. (see picture opposite)

National Style O Resonator

The National Style O, produced from 1930 to 1941, is a single-cone resonator guitar with a steel or brass body, nickel plated and sandblasted with a Hawaiian scene on the back and palm trees on the front and sides. It was built in both squareneck and roundneck styles and the neck joined the body at the 12th fret until 1934 when it joined the body at the 14th fret. For many people the National Style O is instantly recognizable as the guitar on the front cover of Dire Straits' 'Brothers In Arms' album. (see picture on p256)

National Town and Country

The National Town and Country is a deluxe edition 24" scale guitar with three humbucking pickups with individual volume and tone controls above each pickup in a line of six. The lower bout of the body is home to a pickup-selector switch and master volume. The hardware is gold plated to contrast with the wine-to-black sunburst finish. The top of the maple body features a German carve and is bound as is the rosewood fingerboard. The Town and Country guitar sometimes carries the Airline brand name, which was a house brand for the Montgomery Ward catalogue. The guitars were actually made by Valco.

National Tri-cone Style 3

The National Tri-cone Style 3, produced from 1927 to 1942, has two resonator cones on the bass side of the body and one on the treble side. The bridge sits in the center beneath a T-shaped handrest. The metal body is of German silver (i.e. solid nickel alloy with nickel plating) and is decorated with a Lily of the Valley engraving, while the upper part of the body has grid-patterned soundholes. Mahogany roundneck and metal squareneck variants were both available. The bound fingerboard is ebony with diamond shaped inlays, and the slotted headstock sometimes had an ebony veneer and pearl logo.

Normandy Archtop Aluminum Bass

Normandy aluminum archtop guitars are manufactured and hand-riveted in Salem, Oregon. The design pays homage to classic Gibson and Gretsch hollowbodies. The 34" scale Archtop Aluminum Bass is a stunning instrument with its classic singlecut styling finished in either chrome or powder coat with lines of rivets on front and back. The body is constructed of aircraft-grade aluminium, and the hard rock maple neck has a 21-fret rosewood fingerboard. It is fitted with twin Nordstrand humbuckers for high output, midrange and tone, with a volume control for each pickup, a master tone and pickup selector switch.

"Except for a few guitar chords, everything I've learned in my life that is of any value I've learned from women."
- Glenn Frey

Novax Charlie Hunter Semi-hollowbody 8-string

The Charlie Hunter Semi-hollowbody 8-string is effectively a guitar and bass in one with three bass strings and five guitar strings. It features an arched spruce top on a chambered mahogany body. The neck is mahogany with an ebony fingerboard with pearl dot inlays and features the Novax fanned fret system for unsurpassed tuning accuracy, ease of playing, solid, deep bass and rich guitar tone. The guitar has separate custom Bartolini pickups for the bass and guitar strings and a stereo output. An optional set of Graph Tech Ghost piezo pickups provide a sparkling acoustic 8-string tone. (see picture opposite and the Novax CH8 below)

NOVAX
NOVAX
bartolini
bartolini

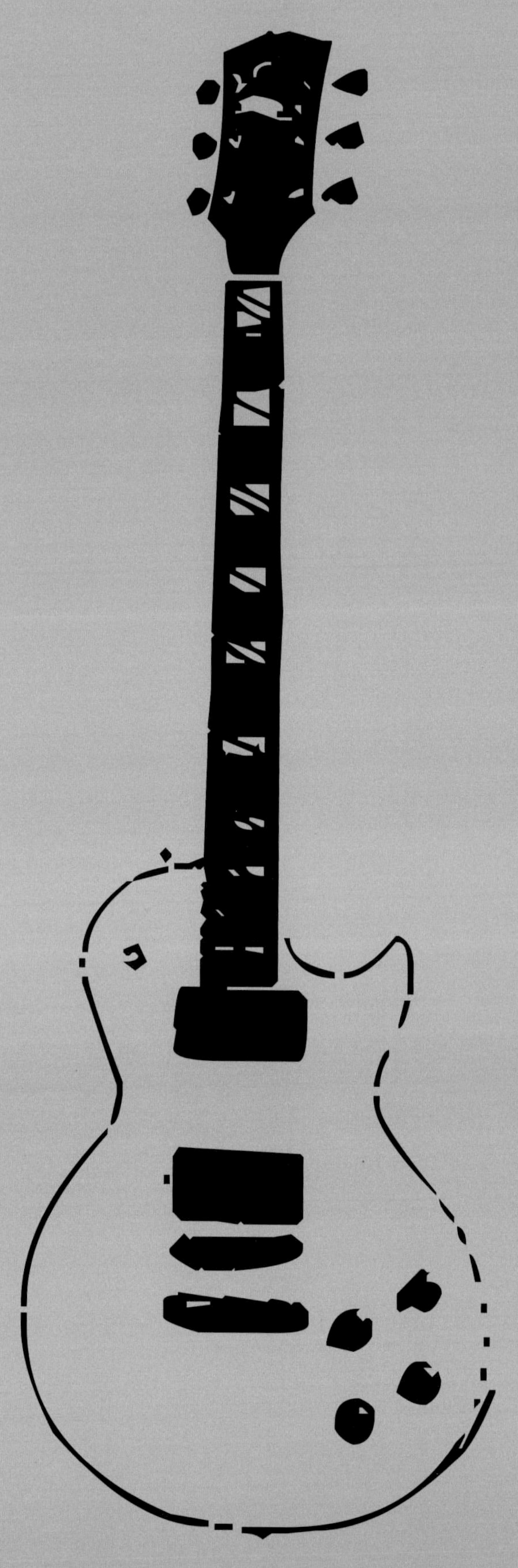

Optek Fretlight Guitar

The Fretlight guitar was developed as an interactive learning tool. Available in several styles including Strat, Tele, Jazzmaster and acoustic models, all feature an advanced polymer fingerboard with LEDs for each string in 21 fret positions. The guitar connects to a computer via a USB cable and in conjunction with the appropriate teaching software the fingerboard illuminates in the relevant positions showing the student where to play, whether it be chords, scales, modes or a melody line. There's no doubt the Fretlight could act as a valuable teaching aid, but complicated electronics mean there's more to go wrong and the longevity of such an instrument is doubtful.

Ormsby Guitars The Shark

Ormsby Guitars of Beaconsfield, Western Australia, have a refreshing 'anything goes' attitude to custom guitar building. The Shark is a semi-hollowbody singlecut design fitted with two humbuckers and wraparound adjustable bridge, volume and tone controls and 3-way switch. The chambered mahogany body has a magnificent quilted maple top finished in aquaburst. The soundhole in the upper bout is cut out in the shape of a hammerhead shark; the effect is like looking down at the ocean and seeing the silhouette of a swimming shark. The set neck is three-piece maple with pin stripes of ebony and has a 24-fret ebony fingerboard inlaid with shark position markers in abalone.

Ovation Adamas

Ovation claims that the Adamas, which debuted in 1976, is the most advanced acoustic guitar ever produced. Its top is made of aerospace-grade graphite in long fibers, designed to respond like spruce but with a third of the mass. Its response is much quicker than an equivalent spruce top, with increased volume and sustain. The top is attached to the bowl of the guitar using a flexible ring as opposed to traditional kerfling, allowing it to vibrate much more freely near the edges. Another innovation is the distinctive multi-soundhole design which requires less bracing so that the top can vibrate more freely. (see picture right)

Ovation Breadwinner

The Breadwinner is sometimes referred to as the first ergonomically designed guitar. Although it was designed specifically to rest comfortably on the knee while seated, the designer's first intention was for it to resemble a medieval battle-axe. The fact that it balances perfectly and supports the right arm can be put down to serendipity. Manufactured in the early-to-mid 1970s by Ovation in New Hartford, Connecticut, the Breadwinner and the slightly more sophisticated Deacon were among the first production guitars (give or take the occasional 1960s Italian oddity) to feature active electronics, having an onboard FET preamp, and were also one of the earliest production guitars to have a 24-fret neck. (see picture left)

Ekrem Özkarpat Classical Fretless

Ekrem Özkarpat is a luthier based in Tünel, Istanbul, Turkey, who hand builds guitars that are purchased by musicians worldwide. He has a reputation for his fretless instruments. Özkarpat's fretless classical guitars are beautifully constructed with body and sides of Honduras mahogany or rosewood, soundboards of cedar, and precisely shaped fingerboards of ebony. The adjustment of the height of the strings is an area where precision is needed. A single millimeter of difference can affect the tone dramatically. Such tonal delicacy is important in a land where music is heard in microtones, and it is perhaps no coincidence that Özkarpat has such an affinity with fretless instruments.

"As a guitar player, you can gravitate to the blues because you can play it easily. It's not a style that's difficult to pick up. It's purely emotive and dead easy to get a start with"
- Boz Scaggs

Palm Guitar

The Palm Guitar is a professional instrument designed primarily as a travel guitar. Built from a composite of fiberglass, graphite and carbon fiber, the guitar has a tiny violin-shaped body. It has a scale length of just over 20" and a total length of 26", and is equipped with a single Seymour Duncan humbucker. which can be selected in series, parallel or singlecoil modes. The headstock is compact, aided by the use of space-saving Linear String Rotation tuners. Unlike the 19" scale Lapstick, which is tuned to A, the Palm Guitar is perfectly happy being tuned to standard pitch with slightly heavier strings.

Parker Fly

The Parker Fly is an innovative electric guitar designed by Ken Parker and Larry Fishman. The guitar is made from various tonewoods set into an extremely rigid exoskeleton made from a composite of carbon fiber, glass and epoxy. This construction makes for a very resonant and lightweight instrument at 4.5lbs. The fingerboard is also made from the same composite and has tangless frets that are quite literally glued on. The Fly uses a combination of magnetic and piezo pickups giving access to electric and acoustic sounds. It also features a high-performance high-tech tremolo system. (see picture left)

Parker P8E Acoustic

The P8E was Parker's first acoustic guitar. In keeping with Parker's reputation established by their electric guitars, this is a high-tech instrument capable of producing a blend of tones from piezo and magnetic pickups. It has a solid flame maple back and sides, a solid cedar top with rosewood binding and a bass-balanced ebony bridge with compensated bone saddle. The neck is made of mahogany with a 19-fret ebony microdot inlaid fingerboard. The electronics are comprised of a Fishman hum-cancelling pickup mounted between the end of the fingerboard and the Selmer-like oval soundhole, and a Fishman Acoustic Matrix undersaddle pickup.

Parkwood PW340FM Acoustic

An elegantly understated acoustic with small white dot fretboard inlays and an open pore finish that lets it resonate freely and retains the feel of raw wood, this simple guitar is made from high quality materials like solid Sitka spruce and solid flamed maple, which stops it from sounding too boomy like other jumbo guitars. Unlike other jumbo guitars, it's also quite easy to handle at a conservative 25.3".

Paul Reed Smith Al Di Meola Prism

Al Di Meola's vibrantly colored signature Prism guitar from PRS is aptly named. The curly maple top probably does not need enhancing with the whole color spectrum splashed across it, but it is nevertheless a very attractive finish. The body is made of mahogany while the neck is Peruvian mahogany with a Black Mexican rosewood fingerboard featuring PRS's trademark "birds" inlay. The pickups are PRS 1957/2008 units and are connected to a volume and push/pull tone and 3-way switch. (see picture on opposite page)

"I have a piano and a guitar, and I tend to switch back and forth between those two instruments to help me get inspired."
- Sean Lennon

AL D

Paul Reed Smith Singlecut Hollowbody Standard

The PRS Singlecut Hollowbody Standard uses mahogany throughout its construction with the exception of a rosewood 22-fret fingerboard inlaid with either moons or abalone birds. Seen from the front the Hollowbody resembles its solidbody sibling apart from the tell-tale f-holes, but viewed from the side it is seen to have a medium-deep body. Electrics are a pair of SC 245 pickups and an optional L.R. Baggs/PRS piezo system incorporated into the stoptail bridge and giving the player access to individual string voicing and real acoustic guitar modeling.

Paul Reed Smith Starla

A single cutaway guitar with a definite retro vibe, this is the first PRS solidbody electric guitar to feature a standard Bigsby B5 tailpiece and a Grove Tune-O-Matic bridge. The solid mahogany body is accented with a 24.5" scale rosewood fingerboard and mahogany neck which create a more subtle finish than other PRS guitars – a highly desirable but unusual piece, from a brand that consistently makes impeccable instruments.

Peavey HP Special USA

The Peavey HP Special USA guitar - named after Peavey's founder and sole owner, Harvey Peavey - is a high-output tone warrior of a guitar. It's armed with coil taps on both custom-wound humbuckers and outfitted with a Floyd Rose tremolo and Peavey's Lok Block system allowing the tremolo to be set fully down or fully floating. The guitar has a 25" scale on a 22-fret oil-finished asymmetrical graphite-reinforced birds eye maple neck. The offset body is made from basswood and is available in flat top and carved top versions. Peavey guitars have pioneered technologies that are now industry standards such as the precise CNC router technology used to shape guitars.

Peavey OCC Custom Guitar

The Peavey OCC Custom Guitar was designed in 2007 in conjunction with Orange County Choppers, a process that was documented in two episodes of the American Chopper TV show. Handcrafted in the Peavey custom shop, the guitar has a batwing meets Explorer-shaped body adorned with a stunning 5A quilted maple top and chrome platework tooled by OCC themselves. The body and set neck are made of mahogany with a 24-fret ebony fingerboard on a 24" scale. Hardware includes Schaller diecast tuners, Tune-o-matic bridge and patented Dual Compression tailpiece, and two custom-wound humbuckers with a volume for each and a master tone.

Peavey Power Slide

Peavey insists that the Power Slide is not a conventional lap steel guitar. As a "next generation slide instrument", it has been ergonomically designed to be played standing up. The body shape is designed to position the fingerboard to the left of the player's body and is held in the correct position by use of a 4-point suspension system and a "Y" strap. The Power Slide also features a unique magnet-loaded pickup with variable coil mode.

Peavey Razer

The Peavey Razer, circa 1983-84, has a very strange body shape that leaves most players perplexed. Some have likened the shape to an electric razor, but it is more akin to a barbed arrowhead or a reverse V with an extra bit stuck on the side for the controls. The guitar is said to be a very good player, although a player who prizes ergonomic builds would be concerned about the lack of right arm support. The guitar features screamingly-hot Super Ferrite twin blade humbuckers with a coil-tapping tone control function, and Peavey's Octave Plus tremolo. (see picture below and another Peavey model being played on opposite page)

Pedulla MVP Bass

Pedulla Basses are completely handmade in Massachusetts by Michael Pedulla. The MVP, with its rounded, almost organic-looking body shape, is based on Pedulla's first design. It is made with through-neck construction producing superb sustain and tone. The body is sculpted from flame maple and the 3-ply maple neck has a fingerboard of ebony with the highest of its 24 frets easily accessible thanks to the depth of the cutaways. The neck has a double-acting truss rod and two steel stiffening bars to maintain stability. The MVP and its fretless counterpart, the Buzz, are available with a choice of pickups and electronics and in 4, 5, 6 and 8-string models.

Peerless PSJ-55CE

Peerless has been building quality archtop and acoustic guitars since 1970, often for other world-renowned brands. The PSJ-55CE is a Super Jumbo Cutaway acoustic guitar with a solid spruce top and laminated mahogany back and sides. The 21-fret neck is made of mahogany and has a rosewood fingerboard with aged white binding and acrylic mother of pearl inlays. The headstock is Peerless' "Lady Lip" shape, which is neatly echoed at the carved rosewood bridge. The guitar features Fishman electronics and has an antique sunburst high-gloss finish.

Peerless Wizard

The Wizard is a striking electric thinline guitar with a 17" wide body of laminated flamed maple in a violin high-gloss finish. The archtop body has aged white/black/mother of pearl binding and a 3-ply black/white/black pickguard. The set-in maple neck has a 20-fret rosewood fingerboard with aged white/black binding and acrylic mother of pearl inlays. The electrics consist of three Dog Ears P90 pickups with individual volume controls and a master tone. The "Lady Lip" style headstock is inlaid with mother of pearl which is triple-bound in aged white/black with mother of pearl which matches the body.

Pignose PGG-100

Pignose is famed for its highly portable mini amplifiers, which despite being only 5 watts sound reasonably good when cranked up. The PGG-100 guitar takes the guts from one of these amps and puts it into a travel guitar. Even though it is a small-bodied guitar it has a full 24" scale on a 22-fret maple neck with rosewood fingerboard. It also features a stacked singlecoil-sized humbucking pickup and a metal Pignose push/pull volume control that also activates the internal 1-watt amp. The speaker is set beneath the strings and has a pseudo-soundhole appearance. It is a guitar that can be played anywhere and can be plugged into something more powerful if required.

Prestige Heritage Hollow

Prestige Guitars are based in Vancouver, Canada, with guitars being built in Korea. They are known for creating guitars with high-quality woods and ornamentation that rival what is commonly used on custom pieces. This true hollowbody features dual f-holes (or s-holes, according to Prestige) and three air slots on the upper bout to provide feedback-free resonance. A massive sustain block under the bridge provides stability, but does not interrupt the sound, while the neck joint is similar to that of a solidbody for more comfortable hand positions. (see the heritage pearl below and the heritage deluxe opposite)

RHYTHM
TREBLE
Bigsby
LICENSED

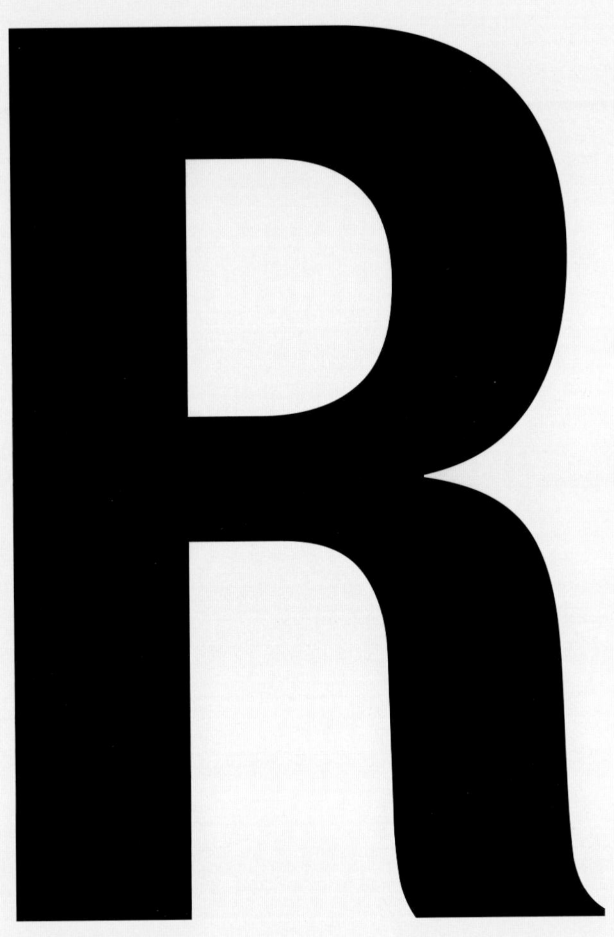

José Ramírez "125 Anos"

José Ramírez III (1922-1995) was the Spanish luthier responsible for major innovations to the classical guitar. He was the grandson of the original José Ramírez, founder of the Ramirez Company. To commemorate the 125th anniversary of the Ramirez guitar-making dynasty, the limited edition "125 Anos" guitar by Amalia Ramírez is based on the high-end "E" model designed by José III. Completely handmade, the back and sides are constructed from solid Indian rosewood and the soundboard is made of solid cedar. The fingerboard is ebony and the guitar is lacquer finished. Its production is strictly for five years only, from 2007 to 2012. (see picture left)

Jose Ramírez 10-string Classical

In 1963, José Ramírez III built a 10-string guitar for Narciso Yepes, but only arrived at the concept after experimenting with a 6-string classical guitar with an additional six sympathetic strings inside the body running through a hollow neck to extra tuners on the head. He gave this guitar to Segovia to try, who was impressed with its sound but insisted that a means was needed to dampen the internal strings during certain passages of music. Ramírez took the problem to Narciso Yepes who initially suggested the untidy solution of using a foot pedal, then later suggested simply adding four strings to neck on the outside of the guitar. Thus the Ramírez 10-string was born.

Raven West Guitars RB7000 7-string Bass

The Raven West RB7000 is a solid ash-bodied bass with a through-neck of hard maple. It also happens to have seven strings. The extra-wide neck has an ebony fingerboard with a vine inlay and other features include Wilkinson tuners, String-Thru string anchoring and active electronics. There has been a growing trend for a number of years in which bassists seem to compete with one another to see who can have the most strings. Basses with 8, 9, 10 and more individual strings are not unheard of, and it begs the question: when does it stop being a bass and become a harp?

Recording King Dreadnaught Gospel Songstress RDC-26

Recording King was originally a house brand for Montgomery Ward in the 1930s with a range of guitars and banjos. Recording King strives to build quality instruments that will last and can be handed down from one generation to the next. The Gospel Songstress is one of their newer models with a top of solid Sitka spruce supported by fully scalloped forward x bracing, and with mahogany back and sides. The one-piece mahogany neck features a Celtic Trinity inlay on the fingerboard and an inlaid Gospel Dove on the head. The tuners are half-moon shaped Grovers.

Red Dog Cigar Box Guitar

In the years after the American Civil War in the Southern Delta there was little money to spend on musical instruments. Any would-be musicians, whether ex-slaves or soldiers, used whatever was available - boxes, tin cans, broom handles, baling, etc to make crude musical instruments. John McNair of Red Dog Guitars specializes in keeping this tradition alive, making resonator, slide, folk, tenor, acoustic and electric cigar box guitars from vintage and antique cigar boxes. They are beautifully made instruments, with fully fretted necks and typically with four strings. McNair insists that you can't create an authentic blues sound on six strings.

"It's the faster bands that made me want to play guitar, bands like The Jam."
- Graham Coxo

Tim Reede Custom Guitars Jazz Standard

Tim Reede builds one-of-a-kind guitars from his workshop in Minnesota. The Jazz Standard is a big-bodied non-cutaway archtop guitar with a 17" wide body and a 25" scale length. It is constructed with AA figured European maple back and sides and an AA European spruce soundboard. Parallel bracing inside the guitar gives it strong projection while maintaining traditional construction. The neck is made from figured maple with fingerboard inlays of gold mother of pearl. The fingerboard, headstock facing, pickguard, tailpiece and binding are all of cocobolo, and the guitar is fitted with a Kent Armstrong suspended pickup.

Reith Custom Mini-HT

Todd Reith of Reith Guitars, based in Denver, Colorado, specializes in building guitars from only the best components. The Mini-HT is a small-bodied headless Tele-type guitar. It has a book-matched 5A grade figured maple flame top on a solid Honduras body with a one-piece graphite neck and fingerboard, which together provide richness, clarity, warmth and sustain. Pickups are Bartolinis mounted in black finished solid brass mounting rings, and electronics include an active Bartolini system with 3-band EQ pre-amp and dual trim pots. The neck is inlaid with flying Vs, and the bridge is Reith's own Sonic Block fixed bridge with tuners.

Reverend Club King RT

Reverend Guitars were founded in 1996 by Joe Naylor, a graduate of the Roberto-Venn School of Luthiery. The Club King is part of Reverend's bolt-on neck series. It is of semi-hollowbody construction with back, sides and center block produced from one slab of korina routed from the top and capped with solid spruce. The neck is maple with a rosewood or maple 22-fret fingerboard. Three different models offer different Reverend-brand pickups: P90s, humbuckers, or Rev-Tron mini-humbuckers. Volume, tone and 3-way switch sit on a Tele-like metal plate while a bass contour control is located near the cutaway.

Seymour Duncan
Seymour Duncan

Reverend Roy Asheton Signature

The Reverend Ron Asheton Signature model was designed for the late Iggy and the Stooges guitarist, based on the V-like Reverend Volcano and built to Asheton's specifications. The korina body has a raised center section which improves clarity and sustain, leaving the thinner body wings to resonant more freely. It has a set, onepiece korina neck with 12" radius rosewood fingerboard, and Wilkinson staggered EZ-Lock tuners. It is fitted with three Reverend P90 pickups with the lead pickup being hotter than usual and the neck and middle pickups being cleaner. Controls are volume, tone and bass contour plus pickup selector.

Rhinehart Guitars Octo-Fish

Billy Rhinehart produces some pretty eccentric guitars. Each is a one-off, hand-carved, hand-painted work of art. Solidbodies are carved out of woods such as mahogany, alder or ash, and are relief carved with pictures varying from fish, birds and dogs to rockets piercing the moon. The Octo-Fish is one such example. It has the neck, pickups and hardware of a Telecaster but there all similarities end. The body is sculpted and brightly painted to show an octopus with its tentacles wrapped around some very unhappy-looking fish.

Rickenbacker Frying Pan

The Electro String Instrument Corporation, based in Los Angeles, was founded in 1931 by Adolph Rickenbacker and George D. Beauchamp. Beauchamp had invented a pickup from two horseshoe magnets and installed it into a simple round wooden body and neck built by Henry Watson. The Frying Pan, the first ever electric guitar, was born. Eager to manufacture the instrument, Beauchamp took it to Adolph Rickenbacker's Tool and Die Shop and together they formed Electro String. The guitars themselves were called "Rickenbacker Electro Instruments" as it was a name the public would latch onto, Rickenbacker's cousin Eddie having been a famous WWI flying ace.

Rickenbacker 331 Lightshow

The Rickenbacker 331LS Light Show, manufactured 1970-75, is similar to the model 330 apart from one special feature: the hollow chambers on each side of the body's solid center section contain colored bulbs and are topped with translucent perspex panels. A control box connects via a 5-pin DIN socket in the side of the guitar while an extra knob near the tailpiece controls the light circuit. The guitar is illuminated with red, yellow and blue lights depending on the pitch of the notes being played. A bass version of this psychedelic guitar, the 4005LS Bass, was also produced, and The Byrds' Roger McGuinn is thought to have the only 12-string example, the 341LS.

Rickenbacker Model B Lap Steel

After the Frying Pan, one of the most popular Rickenbacker Electro Instruments was the Model B Hawaiian guitar. It was made out of Bakelite, and the five chrome plates set into the top of the guitar and single volume control can identify early examples. By the late 1930s the plates were white-enamelled and a tone control had been added. A Bakelite Model B Spanish guitar with detachable neck was introduced in 1935. Guitarists found that although the body was much smaller than that of the archtops to which they were accustomed, it suffered none of the feedback problems.

Rickenbacker 4001 Bass

The 4001, originally created in 1961, is the most popular of the Rickenbacker basses. Featuring the "crested wave" body shape, its construction is unusual for a bass of its vintage because it uses through-neck construction, meaning the neck goes all the way through the body. Rickenbacker basses have a very distinctive sound, and the 4001 is no exception. Loved by Lemmy from Motörhead and Peter Quaife of The Kinks, this is another enduring favorite.
(see picture opposite)

Rickenbacker

Rim Custom Marseer 5-string Bass

Rim basses are built by Robbie McDade in the UK. The Custom Marseer 5-string Bass, crafted from exotic timbers, is a beauty to behold from its slotted head right down to the fishtail where the strings are anchored. It has a five-piece neck of purpleheart and wenge with an ebony fingerboard, bubinga body wings, and a stunning cocobolo bookmatched top. Pickups are Haeussel Jazzbucker and singlecoil units faced with ebony, and other hardware includes Hipshot Ultralite tuners, ETS Mk3 bridge and custom tailpiece, and an Aguilar or Noll preamp. (see picture below)

RISA Guitar Solid

RISA Musical Instruments, based in Germany, specialisze in ukuleles, although they have occasionally produced guitars. The Guitar Solid is a curious-looking instrument resembling a cricket bat with a large hole in the front. It is a travel guitar with a headless design and minimal body. The strings pass over the bridge, around a roller to the rear of the instrument and then to a row of six banjo-style non-geared tuners in the top edge of the body. The pickup is a passive Shadow piezo and so the guitar can be fitted with steel or nylon strings.

RKS Chrome Molly

RKS Guitars, designed by industrial designer Ravi Sawhney working with musician Dave Mason, takes a completely different approach to the hollowbodied guitar. Inspired by the skeletal human form, the RKS has a unique open architecture. The body section is made from a wood-based polymer and is connected to the core section by aluminium alloy ribs, creating an uncommon resonance and detail. The through-neck core is made from maple and alder and has an ebony 22-fret fingerboard, together providing clarity and sustain. Volume and tone controls are wheels in the core's underside and the pickup selector is located on the top. The Chrome Molly has a mirror-finish, and is the model played by Daniel Ash from Bauhaus.

Roadrunner Surfin' Bird

Roadrunner Guitars, based in Nancy, France, are the creations of Laurent Hassoun. Models produced are a mixed bag of the familiar, the retro and the crazy, and have been played by the likes of Lee Ranaldo (Sonic Youth), Billy Childish and Bo Diddley. The Surfin' Bird guitar is a semi-hollow design based on the shape of a surfboard. It has two humbuckers, volume, tone and 3-way switch, with two curved soundholes on the upper half complementing the guitar's shape. A pair of inwardly-curving horns may possibly hinder higher fret access, so perhaps this is a guitar for rhythm players rather than widdlers. (see picture below)

Rob Williams CS Carved Top

Rob Williams has been building guitars since 1984 and his career has included working for both Jaydee and Patrick Eggle in the UK. Made in Great Britain, the Rob Williams CS Carved Top range of guitars takes the familiar Stratocaster-style guitar and gives it a makeover. Options include a standard model with all mahogany construction, a deluxe model with a high-grade maple top, and a swamp ash model. Hardware includes Gotoh tuners, Hipshot hardtail bridge or Wilkinson tremolo, and Rob Williams' own pickups.

Roberts Roto Neck

Looking at the Roberts Roto-Neck guitar you are unsure whether this design is one of genius or if it is simply barking mad. It has two fingerboards on two different faces of the same neck. The guitar is designed so that both fingerboards - effectively two guitars – can be played simultaneously. The left-hand plays barre chords (presumably using an open chord tuning) using the thumb on the upper fingerboard as the fingers play the melody on the forward-facing fingerboard, while the right hand's thumb strums the chord and its fingers pluck the lead.

Robin Fleetwood Exotic

Robin Guitars are handcrafted in Houston, Texas. The Fleetwood Exotic is reminiscent of Gibson's Firebird with a longer, pointier lower horn, and including the raised center body section. The body is built from solid mahogany and has a figured maple face with grained ivoroid binding. The one-piece mahogany set-neck has a rosewood fingerboard with 22 jumbo frets and mother of pearl inlay dots. The headstock is a split fishtail design with Grover tuners arranged four on the top and two on the bottom. Rio Grande pickups have separate volume controls, a master tone and a 3-way pickup selector.

Robin Octave Guitar

The Robin Octave Guitar dates to the mid-1980s and is a Strat-type guitar with a half-scale neck and an upside-down banana headstock. It is tuned a whole octave above standard tuning. Known players include session guitarist Tommy Tedesco, Dave Stewart of The Eurythmics, Charlie Burchill of Simple Minds, and the Vaughan brothers Jimmy and Stevie Ray who simultaneously played a Robin doubleneck with standard and octave necks.
(see Robin guitar below)

Roland G77 Bass Guitar Synth Controller

In the 1980s the Roland Corporation's experiments with guitar synthesizers met with varying levels of success. The aim was to give guitarists access to the same range of sounds as keyboard players. Guitar-based synth controllers had a divided pickup with separate outputs for each string allowing each note to be sent via an analogue-to-digital converter and used to generate a tone. The G77 was the bass companion model to the Roland G-707 guitar synth, and is considered superior in that it has individual analogue-to-digital converters for each string, unlike the guitar which had one for all six, and so the tracking was vastly improved. It also had a slightly more sensibly designed shape so that you could actually play it sitting down.

Royal Electra Mk II

The Electra Mk II is the best known guitar manufactured by Kevin Chilcott of Royal Guitars in the UK. Shaped like a Strat with pointed horns, it more noticeably has a series of 15 decorative holes routed through the body. The design was influenced by a modified Strat used by Russ Ballard of Argent, who was in turn inspired by the holey metal chairs popular in the early 1970s. Chilcott claims that the Electra was the first guitar to feature a pickup selector going through a slot in the guitar body rather than being mounted through a pickguard, that it was the first to employ a humbucker-sized P90 pickup, and also that it was the first to angle a humbucker in the bridge position. (see picture opposite)

"Among God's creatures two, the dog and the guitar, have taken all the sizes and all the shapes, in order not to be separated from the man."
- Andres Segovia

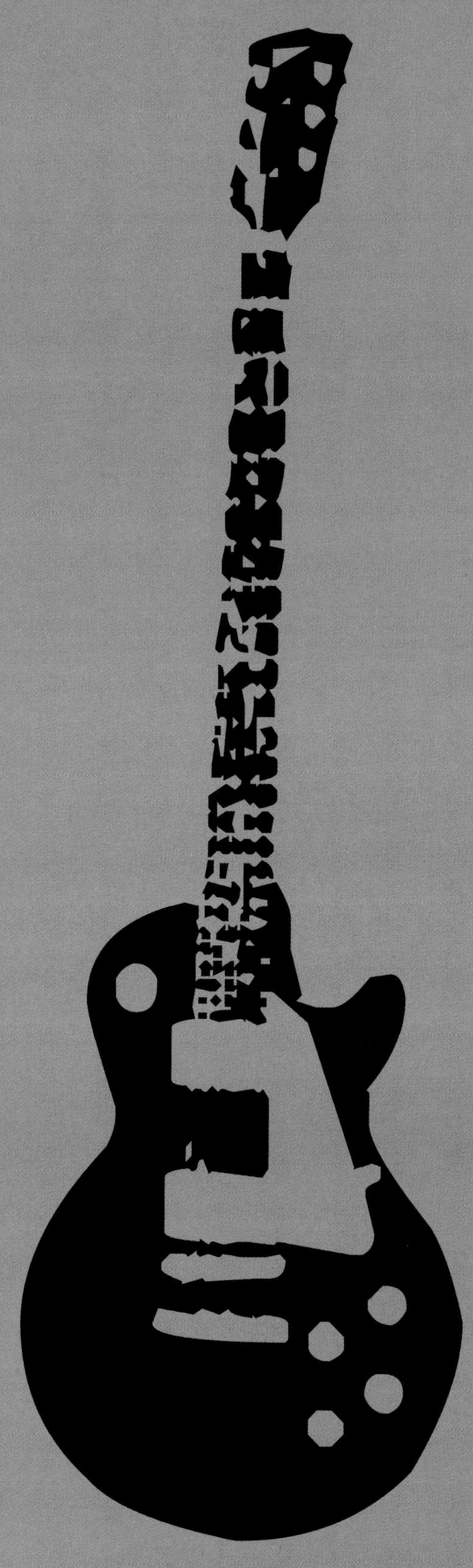

Sadowsky P/J 5-string Bass

Sadowsky Guitars from Brooklyn, New York, has been making high-quality guitars and basses since 1979. Sadowsky basses are meticulously crafted custom shop instruments based on the Fender Jazz Bass. The Metro series MVP-P/J is a 5-string bass with a slim Jazz Bass-like body built from swamp ash and finished in a 3-tone sunburst. The neck and fingerboard are maple with a 12" radius and measuring 1 7/8" at the nut. The bass features Sadowsky P/J pickups and has an onboard pre-amp with vintage tone control. A similar bass is also available in the even more exclusive New York City series.

Saint Blues 61 South

Founded in 1983 by Tom Keckler, Saint Blues Guitars are based in Memphis, Tennessee. With a semi-legendary status among those in the know, they look something like a sawn-down Telecaster but with tapped coil pickups they have many more tonal options, while the body shape offers comfort and balance. The 61 South has a small Tele-like body with an acoustic chamber and f-hole. It is available with dual-tapped singlecoil St. Blues pickups or with a P90 at the neck and tapped singlecoil at the bridge. The ash body is double bound and the neck is made from a single piece of hard rock maple. (see picture below)

Salomon "Harpolyre" Triple Neck, 1830

The Harpolyre was patented in 1829 by Jean Francois Salomon, a music teacher in Besançon, France. It would typically be crafted from mahogany and ebony with bone nuts and bridge saddles. It has the appearance of a triple-necked guitar but only the middle 6-string neck is played in guitar fashion. The top neck carries "chromatic" sub-bass strings and the lower neck has "diatonic" mid-range strings. Even though the outer two necks are fretted they are not intended for left-handing fingering; the strings would be played open, harp-style. The presence of frets is mainly for aesthetic purposes.

Schecter Genesis

The Schecter Genesis has an Explorer-like body with cut-out "tone holes" and is believed to have been inspired by the Guild X-100 Blade Runner. Looking at the two guitars side by side it can be seen that there are too many similarities between the designs for this to be mere coincidence. The guitar has a 22-fret neck, two humbuckers with volume, tone and 3-way pickup selector, and a locking tremolo. The hardware is chrome-plated.

Schecter Ultracure

The Schecter Ultracure is the signature model for Robert Smith of The Cure, and was designed with input from Smith himself. It is a 25 1/2" scale set-neck design with a slightly oversized body of mahogany featuring a raised center section. The neck is also mahogany and has a rosewood 24-fret fingerboard inlaid with black pearl "stars and moons" position markers. Pickups are a Seymour Duncan 1959 set, controlled via a volume for each pickup with push/pull coil tapping, a master volume and a 3-way pickup selector. The bridge is a TonePros TOM system and the Grover tuners are arranged on the headstock in a 2+4 formation.

Friedrich Schenk, Lyra-Bassguitar, Vienna about 1850

The Lyra-Bassguitar by Friedrich Schenk and dating from around 1850 is from the private collection of R. Krause. It is built in the style of a lyre guitar with the two outer arms extending out until they merge with the headstock. Unlike most lyre guitars, the Lyra-Bassguitar has an additional four sub-bass strings on the bass side of the instrument, which places this instrument into the realm of harp guitars. The guitar is bound and ornately carved, particularly around where the arms meet the hollow headstock. The headstock is particularly interesting as it has its own soundhole.

Scherzer 10-string guitar, 1862

Johan George Scherzer was an apprentice to the famed Viennese luthier Stauffer at the same time as C.F. Martin was serving his own apprenticeship. Unlike Martin, who went to America to seek his fortune, Scherzer stayed on in Vienna and eventually inherited his master's business. The Scherzer guitar has a second "neck" carrying four sub-bass strings. These are tuned ABCD, the tuning referred to as "Romantic" or sometimes "Baroque". The fretted six-string neck has a fingerboard that extends up to a 24th fret. An iron bar is fitted inside the body to aid rigidity and take the pressure off the spruce top.

J. Schuster, Terz guitar, 1845

The Terz guitar is a short-scale guitar pitched at a minor third higher than a regular guitar, which gives it a clear tone that carries well. Terz guitars were not known to have been used for solo pieces. They were popular in ensemble situations and guitar duos, etc. Mauro Giuliani composed extensively for the Terz guitar as a compliment to the prime guitar. The Terz guitar by J.Schuster, dating from around 1845, in the collection of Bernhard Kresse, is built in the style of Stauffer. It has maple back and sides with a top of spruce and a scale length of 22".

Domenico Sellas, 1670

The guitar by Domenico Sellas of Venice, circa 1670, is part of the collection of the National Music Museum, The University of South Dakota in Vermillion. It is a 10-string guitar with strings paired into five courses. Its spruce top is inlaid with ebony, ivory and mother of pearl, while the fingerboard inlays are of incised mother of pearl plaques. The back and sides are made of snakewood and feature ivory stringing, which gives a striped effect. The neck and headstock are of ebony and feature ornate figures and foliage carved from ivory. The overall length of the guitar is 33".

Selmer Maccaferri "D-hole"

The Selmer Maccaferri D-hole guitar is a large-bodied instrument with a squared single cutaway. Strings pass over a moveable bridge to a tailpiece as they would on an archtop. The top of the guitar is sometimes lightly arched, but this is achieved by bending the wood rather than through carving. The fingerboard is of classical width, and the headstock is slotted as on a classical guitar. The large D shaped soundhole was conceived to house an internal resonator devised by Mario Maccaferri, although it did not prove popular and examples rarely still have this feature.

Selmer "Oval-hole"

As soon as it became available circa 1935, the oval-hole Selmer was Django Reinhardt's guitar of choice. Produced after Maccaferri's involvement with Selmer had ended, the oval-hole guitar differs from its predecessor in that its longer scale allows it to be played harder and its smaller oval hole makes the sound more directional and much better at projecting. Its loud and cutting sound is still popular today with the lead players in Django-style bands while rhythm players might use the D-hole guitar. Selmer guitars were usually of laminated Indian rosewood with walnut necks. Tops were always solid spruce. (see 1939 Selmer advert, opposite)

AUX MEILLEURS ARTISTES...
LES MEILLEURS INSTRUMENTS

4

Selsam Hellrazor Tarantula Bass

The Hellrazor Tarantula Bass is a spider-shaped bass built by Doug Selsam of Fullerton, California, and is said to have been constructed using a unique manufacturing process. The body has a thick maple core beneath its proprietary composite structure, while the neck is of birdseye maple with a 22-fret African ebony fingerboard. The bass is fitted with Seymour Duncan APJ-1 Active EQ pickups, which contribute to its deep and piano-like tone. As good as it may sound, this bass is not recommended to those suffering from arachnophobia.

Shergold Doubleneck

Shergold Guitars was founded in 1967 by Jack Golder and Norman Houlder who had previously worked for Burns Guitars. They produced instruments for various other brands until 1975 when they launched their own brand name. They are particularly well known for their doublenecks. Most famously, Mike Rutherford of Genesis played a Shergold doubleneck. What is not generally known is that his doubleneck was modular and actually consisted of four individual guitar sections that could be clipped together. The bottom neck was always a bass, which could be paired with one of two different 12-strings (for different tunings) and a six-string.
(see picture opposite)

Shergold Modulator

A classic British-built instrument, the Shergold Modulator is testament to the spirit of ingenuity and innovation of the small independent manufacturers. The guitar, with a slab body of selected kiln-dried hardwood and a bolt-on neck of Canadian hard rock maple, features interchangeable electronics modules producing different sounds for different situations. There are eight modules, namely: Basic, Phasing, Bypass, Stereo, Recording, Quad, Booster and Designer.
For example, the Basic module provides Telecaster-type switching, whereas the Bypass module has Les Paul switching (plus an option to completely bypass the volume and tone circuits).
It was the Variax of its day!

Shergold

Sho-Bud Spade Model Acoustic

Sho-Bud, known for its pedal steel guitars, branched out in the 1970s with a Japanese-made series of acoustic guitars based on the Martin Dreadnought. The suits from a pack a cards - diamonds, clubs, hearts and spades – were printed on the necks of their steels, and this iconography continued through to the acoustic guitars. There were five models: the Club, the Diamond, the Heart, the Spade and the Grand Slam. They featured the hearts, diamonds, clubs and spades position markers and a large inlay of the particular model on the headstock. These guitars earned themselves an excellent reputation but are now very hard to find.

Sho-Bud Pro III

The Sho-Bud Pro III Custom is a doubleneck pedal steel with eight floor pedals, four knee levers and aluminium necks. Each neck has 10 strings, with dual coil pickups allowing sound selection. The body is of solid birdseye maple for finest sustaining quality and has a highly polished, hand-rubbed lacquer finish. The end plates, keyheads, tail plates and pedal bar are all of polished aluminium. Tuners are Grover Rotomatics and a patented roller bridge mechanism can raise or lower any string. The top neck is tuned to E9 and is operated with pedals 1, 2 and 3, while the bottom neck is tuned to C6 and operated with pedals 4, 5, 6, 7 and 8. The knee levers operate the E9 neck, with the R/L lever operating on both.

"I sit down and create atmospheres, start playing guitar or piano and just sing whatever comes out of my mouth."
- Martin Gore

Siggy Braun Little Crow

Siggy Braun Guitars are based in Western Germany. The Little Crow is a luxurious original asymmetrical design with a wave-shaped upper horn. The guitar features Siggy Braun's innovative CNS-System deep-set bolt-on neck. It has an alder body topped with a carved AAAAA-grade quilted maple top, and a pau ferro neck with a 24-fret ebony fingerboard featuring abalone crow inlays. The matching headstock has fake binding and a 2+4 tuner layout. Hardware includes Schaller locking tuners, Schaller Floyd Rose 2 tremolo, and two of Siggi's own pickups with master volume and master tone switches. Finally, the guitar is finished in a Crow Burst high gloss.

Siegmund Resolectric

Sigmund Guitars of California were established in 1993 and are custom built by Chris Sigmund. The Sigmund Resolectric is a hybrid of a resonator, acoustic and electric jazz guitar. It shares the same shape as Sigmund's archtop guitars with a wide exaggerated lower body bout. The body is made of laminated walnut and the neck is made from one piece of mahogany with an ebony fingerboard with dot inlays and 22-frets. The Quarterman handspun resonator cone is mounted so that its vibrations blend with the guitar's top. The guitar features a lipstick pickup in the neck position and a built-in EV microphone element, which are wired to a stereo output. (see pictures opposite)

Silvertone 1448L "Amp In Case"

The Silvertone 1448L was first sold in Sears, Roebuck & Co's stores in 1963. It was a simple guitar with a single lipstick pickup and was finished in black metalflake. When Danelectro's Nathan Daniel had been trying to seal the deal to supply Sears with guitars for the Silvertone range, the Sears buyer J.N Fisher insisted on an accompanying amplifier, and so the guitar came in a carrying case that had a 3-watt amplifier and a 6" speaker built in. To cut costs, the guitars were assembled cheaply with bodies being made of masonite stapled to a poplar frame. (see picture on p310)

Sorbera Amara

Sorbera Guitars, based in Bulverde, Texas, was started almost by accident when the Sorbera brothers were left their grandfather's workshop after he passed away. When one brother wanted to learn the guitar they decided to build one rather than buy a cheap and inferior instrument. However, they got carried away with their choice of timbers, and one guitar led to another and so it grew into a business. The Amara is a lightweight, comfortable solid electric built from quality tonewoods of the customer's choice. Tight build tolerance and a deep set-neck create a resonant guitar with long sustain and clarity.

Specimen "Maccaferri"

Specimen is based in Chicago and builds custom guitars, tube amplifiers and audio horns. Handcrafted by Ian Schneller, guitars are usually made from traditional materials but sometimes unusual materials such as phenolic, aluminium, bell brass and masonite are used. The "Maccaferri" guitar borrows the Selmer gypsy guitar shape and renders it in aluminium. (The Maccaferri name is a misnomer as evidenced by the oval soundhole). It has a full acoustic body, birdseye maple neck with aluminium facing on the headstock and a 22-fret ebony fingerboard. It is fitted with a mini-humbucker in the neck position and a transducer in the bridge and is wired for stereo output.

Rolf Spuler Paradis

The Rolf Spuler Paradis was conceived as "a stage-friendly guitar, staying true to its natural sound at any volume level, for nylon and steel strings alike". The single cutaway body has a tuned cavity enhancing the acoustic properties and features two faux sound holes that pass right through the body. The neck is made of solid rosewood and has 24 frets, which are narrowed from the 12th position upwards for precise intonation. The tuners are modified Gotohs while the E-string has a D-tuner and a 2-fret fingerboard extension. The guitar uses Spuler's own piezo pickup system and state-of-the-art electronics.

Squier STRATOCASTER
Squier Fender TELECASTER

Squier '51

By the late 1970s, Fender was facing competition from Japanese brands such as Tokai and Greco, and launched the Squier brand to produce their own budget guitars. Production soon moved to Japan, and later to Korea, China and other countries. The Squier '51 guitar is one of its few models not based on a Fender original. Its design borrows from the Tele, Strat and '51 Precision Bass, with a singlecoil pickup in the neck position and a humbucker at the bridge. The controls are volume with coil tap and 3-postion pickup selector. The guitar was produced from 2004 to 2006 and has become a favorite among modders. (see picture left)

Squier Hello Kitty Stratocaster

The Squier Hello Kitty Stratocaster saw Fender jumping on the guitars-for-girls bandwagon started by the likes of Daisy Rock. The Hello Kitty Stratocaster has an agathis body and a C-shaped maple neck with 21-fret maple fingerboard. The body is finished in pink or black and features a shaped pickguard depicting the Hello Kitty cartoon character, while the Hello Kitty logo is on the back of the guitar. It has a single humbucker in the bridge position, a single volume control, and a hardtail bridge.

"I learned to play guitar at a young age and converted poems and stuff that I had written to songs."
- Gregory Harrison

Status Graphite S2-Classic Headless Bass

Rob Green of Essex, UK, has been building basses since the early 1980s. The Status Graphite Series 2 was first produced in 1983 and its design uses a combination of woven carbon graphite and exotic woods. The earliest examples had a headless graphic through-neck construction with body wings of exotic woods. The range was later expanded to include bolt-on neck models, headed basses, and 5 and 6-string variants. The S2 has an active circuit that provides a wide range of tonal options. Master volume and pickup blend control are standard, while controls allowing bass and treble cut/boost and a variable frequency midrange are optional.

Status Graphite Electro-4 Bass

The Electro 4 is an up-to-date design from Status Graphite. The bass features a deep-set woven graphite neck fitted to a chambered body of mahogany with a book-matched rosewood top and a single f-hole. The graphite neck provides sustain and clarity while the chambered body makes the bass highly resonant; together with the piezo pickup in the bridge, Hyperactive magnetic pickup and a two-band EQ, a vast combination of tones is available. As if this was not enough the bass is available with four or five strings and in fretted and fretless options.

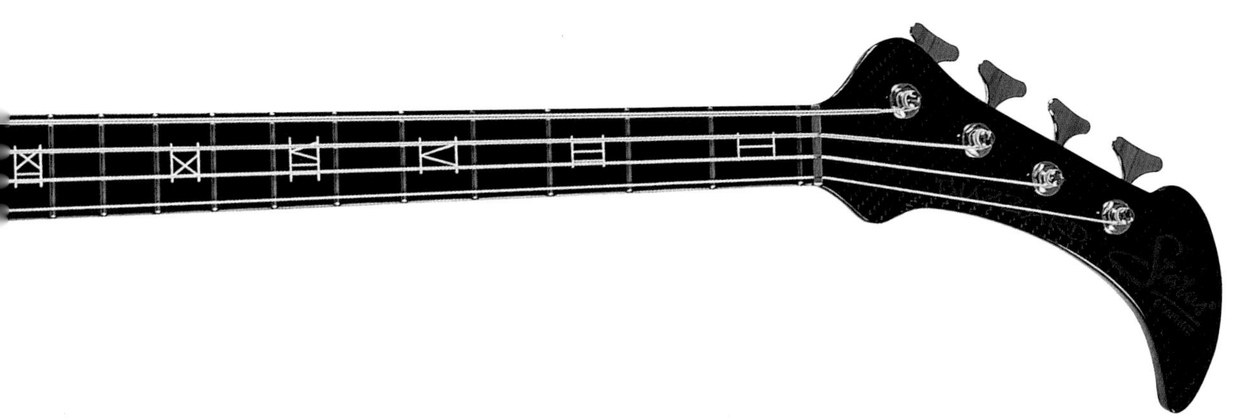

"If you've got a guitar and a lot of soul, just bang something out and mean it. You're the superstar."
- Krist Novoselic

Steinberger Demon

Steinberger seems to have taken a leaf out of BC Rich's book with the design of the Demon. It does not have the appearance of a guitar you would feel comfortable with playing any other music than metal. It is a hybrid guitar combining the rigidity and clarity of graphite with the warmth of wood. The Cybrosonic through-neck is hardrock maple around a graphite U-shaped channel and adjustable trussrod, and is topped with a phenolic fingerboard. Pickups are two EMGs and a piezo-equipped bridge. The guitar has a baritone 28 5/8" scale, but use of a clever built-in capo allows regular guitar tuning among other options.

Steinberger L-series Bass

The Steinberger L-series Bass, first produced in New York in 1979, is an innovative design that spawned a huge number of imitations. The bass is made from a blend of graphite and carbon fiber for rigidity, strength and great sustain. The whole design is minimalist. The body is a small rectangular shape while the neck is headless. It's as if the bass had been stripped down to its bare essentials. The radical design coupled with the use of low-impedance EMG pickups made for a sonically clean sounding instrument, which perfectionists loved and traditionalists hated. (see picture opposite)

Stepp DGX

The Stepp DGX is not a true guitar, but a guitar-like synthesizer controller. The guitar has two sets of strings, one on the fretboard and used to determine pitch and string bends, and a trigger set on the body used for picking or strumming. Each string can be assigned its own parameters and MIDI channel so that different strings can trigger different synth sounds. Other functions include the ability to sustain a chord or note while playing over the top. This was one guitar synth controller that actually did what it said on the tin. However, that didn't stop it sinking almost without trace.

Stevens Guitars Guit-Steel

Junior Brown, a country guitarist and singer from Cottonwood, Arizona, famously plays a hybrid doubleneck guitar known as the Guit-Steel. Built by Michael Stevens of Stevens Guitars, the guitar features a Tele-style neck and a lap steel neck. The original, "Old Yeller", used the guitar neck from Brown's Fender Bullet, but subsequent models have used Tele-style necks with the profile laser-copied from the original. The body with its Fender Stringmaster styling is made from ash with chrome-plated pickguards and an aluminium fingerboard for the steel neck. Brown's own Guit-Steels make use of Sho-Bud pickups on both necks.

Stevens Guitars Slant 6 Bass

The Slant 6 Bass from Stevens Guitars has a 34" scale, a body made of alder, and neck made from quarter-sawn hard rock maple with a 24-fret fingerboard. The neck has a graphite stabilizer with adjustable truss rod and measures 2 3/8" at the nut and 3" at the body. The humbucking pickups are Stevens' own and are set into the body at a rakish slant. The headstock is Fender-like and has Ultralight tuners by Hipshot arranged in a 4+2 layout. The bass is produced in set-neck and bolt-on versions and is finished in Nitrocellulose lacquer.

Stewart Guitars The Stowaway

The Stowaway by Stewart Guitar is a Strat-style guitar with a detachable headless neck that can be stored in a diagonal recess in the back of the guitar's body. The whole guitar then fits into a carry case, which is roughly the size of an attache case. The detachable neck uses Stewart Guitar's patented Clip-Joint, which allows the neck to be detached quickly and easily without using tools, but when fully assembled the guitar has the excellent sustain and stability you'd expect from a professional instrument.

STHAC Guitars Virtuoso Sustainer SL 24

STHAC produces tailor-made and hand-finished guitars in Tacoma, Washington, and in their custom shop in Noiseau, France. Their Virtuoso Sustainer model is the most evolutionary model in their catalogue. The body is made of a single piece of US alder with a maple top. The neck is flamed US AAA-grade hard rock maple with a 24-fret African ebony fingerboard. The guitar features DiMarzio pickups and a Fernandes Sustainer for infinite sustain effects. It also features a Speedloader Floyd-Rose locking nut and bridge which effectively render the guitar's headstock obsolete, although it does have a sleek headstock for aesthetical purposes.

Andy Stone "Les Pew"

Andy Stone's Les Pew has a hollow body built from antique pine from a Victorian pew purchased from his local church. The body is bound and features herringbone purfling to hide the join between top and back. The one-piece maple neck and fingerboard has the truss rod inserted from the rear and a skunk stripe made from the leg of a school chair. The front and back of the body retain the original 1858 pew finish. The guitar is fitted with a humbucker in the neck position and a singlecoil in the bridge position, and although initially not sure about the tonal properties of antique pine, Andy describes the sound as "stunning".

Stradivarius 5-course Guitar, 1700

Stradivarius, the world famous violin maker, is also known to have made guitars such as an example dated 1700 in the collection of the National Music Museum in South Dakota. This is a 5-course guitar, i.e. with ten strings in pairs. Guitar strings were doubled to give a fuller and louder sound when played chordally. Tuning difficulties and the problems in playing rapid passages may well have been causes for the switching over to single strings in the years following the introduction of the 6-course guitar, circa 1750. Oxford University's Ashmolean Museum has an earlier example of a Stradivarius guitar, dated 1688. (see picture on p321)

Stroh Guitar

The Strohviol was created by John Matthias Augustus Stroh in the early 20th Century. The phono or horned instruments that he created, most commonly violins, were designed to produce a sharper, more directional sound to assist recording on wax cylinders. The Stroh guitar has a 6-string neck mounted on a minimal body with the bridge positioned over a diaphragm. The sound from the guitar would be transmitted through this diaphragm and projected out of a large horn which would be pointed towards the microphone. This is believed to have been the source of John Dopyera's resonator guitar concept.

Stromberg Master 400

The archtop Master 400 was Stromberg's top-of-the-line model in the 1940s. Built by Elmer Stromberg of Charles A Stromberg and Son, Boston, these guitars became increasingly popular with jazz musicians. The Master 400 was an immensely powerful guitar, and with a non-cutaway 19-inch wide body it was larger than even Gibson's Super 400. In fact, it is said to be the largest and loudest acoustic guitar ever built. Legendary rhythm guitarist Freddie Green used a Stromberg Master 400 to cut through the sound of Count Basie's band.

"But remember, guitar players are a dime a dozen."
- Krist Novoselic

Stromberg Newport Non-Cutaway

The Stromberg name was resurrected in the 2000s by Larry Davis, who works for WD Music Products, which sells guitar parts. The guitars themselves are manufactured in Korea and fitted with parts from WD. The Newport model has back and sides of maple, a laminated maple top with multi-layer laminate binding on the body and neck. It has a scale length of 24" and the body is 16" at its widest point. The guitar is fitted with a Kent Armstrong side-mounted Jazz Slimbucker with a hidden volume control under the pickguard. Tuners are Kluson Deluxe with pearloid tulip buttons.

Strobel Rambler

Strobel Guitars manufactures high-end electric travel guitars. With a small body and a headless neck the Rambler is already compact but if you need to pack it into an even smaller space it dismantles into neck and body sections that easily fit inside your briefcase. A handy StringKeeper gadget even keeps the strings in order when the Rambler is dismantled. Bodies are built of mahogany or ash and have a flame maple top. The Rambler is fitted with a pair of Schaller Gold 50 humbuckers with separate volume and tone controls. The Tune-o-matic bridge and locking tuners (located in a V in the base of the body) are also by Schaller. (see picture below)

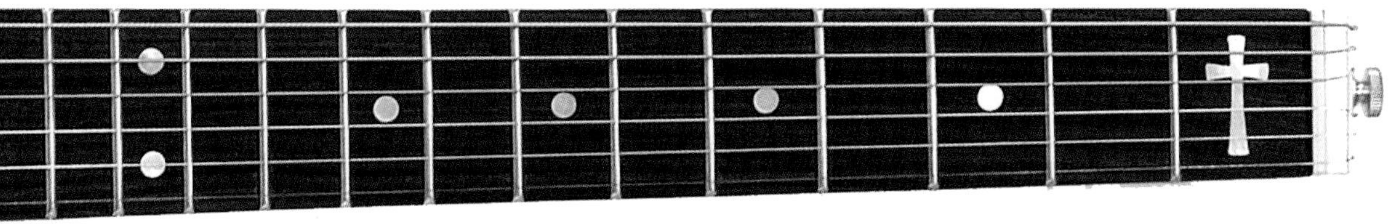

"A wah-wah is important as well. I love it; it makes the guitar scream." - Robin Trower

Suhr Pro Series M1

Suhr guitars are boutique instruments built in California using the latest technologies. Necks, bodies and pickguards are cut on CNC (Computer Numeric Control) routers, but made to feel like hand-built guitars. The M1 has been called the best 24-fret bolt-on guitar on the market in 2009. It has a sleek modern body of alder with a contoured heel for high fret access. The fast maple neck has an elliptical shape with a pau ferro or maple neck. The pickups are Suhr's own humbuckers and the guitar features switch allowing both singlecoil and humbucker sounds to be accessed. (see right, and the Suhr Strat on p324)

Supersound Type 2

Supersound Electronic Products, formed by Alan and Mary Wootton in 1952, was a small British company producing electronic goods such as turntables, tape recorders and instrument amplifiers from 1952 to 1974. They branched into guitar production and their Ike Isaacs Short Scale guitar is thought to have been the first commercially available British-built electric guitar. The Supersound Type 2, made in 1959-60, is a short scale guitar with a 23" scale and is made from Pyrana pine. It has two Supersound pickups and a neck with wide block markers.

"The guitar is a much more efficient machine than a computer. More responsive." - Colin Greenwood

Supro
Dual Tone

Supro Dual Tone

The Supro Dual Tone, manufactured by Valco in the mid 1950s, is a rather innocuous-looking single cutaway guitar finished in a white plastic coating with black and white bi-level pickguard and controls. It has two pickups that look like humbuckers but are actually singlecoils. The baseball bat-shaped neck has a 20-fret rosewood fingerboard and no truss rod. A screw on the back adjusts neck angle. The guitar is known for its fat sounding neck pickup, and vicious sounding bridge pickup with the tone rolled off, and has been played by Link Wray, Jimmy Page and David Bowie. (see David Bowie playing the Dual Tone below)

Supro Folkstar Resonator

The Supro Folkstar is a resonator guitar from the 1960s with a single cone set in a thin "Res-o-glas" fibreglass body. The body is constructed in two halves, the join of which is hidden beneath the plastic edge binding. In retrospect, the choice of body material has not been considered a successful one given the acoustic nature of the guitar. However, seeing as it is a resonator instrument, the lo-fi quality of the guitar's voice does have a certain charm and can be particularly suited to blues and slide playing.

Switch Revolution X101

Switch Guitars first appeared in 2003 and are, sadly, almost a memory. They were molded in one piece from a revolutionary new material called Vibracell, a polyurethane resin that the makers claim has a similar consistency to mahogany. The Revolution model is clearly based on the design of the Burns Flyte. It has two humbuckers, a Tune-o-matic bridge, and Grover tuners. Its 3-dimensional molded body features deep chambered rear body grooves and is said to be remarkably resonant and, combined with the hot pickups, produces a radical sustain.

Switch Stein IV

The Switch Stein IV also has a one-piece body molded from Vibracell. It features a double cutaway design with a 22-fret rosewood fingerboard inlaid with pearl crown position markers. Pickups are a pair a ceramic humbuckers with volume control for each plus a master tone and a 3-way pickup selector switch. Other hardware includes a roller saddle tremolo bridge and Grover tuners. The body is highly contoured and shaped with the controls inset at a lower level where they cannot be accidentally knocked.

Synsonics Terminator

The Synsonics Terminator, despite its grandiose name, is a short scale small-bodied guitar with a roughly approximated Strat-like shape, two singlecoil pickups, tremolo, and a built-in amp and speaker powered by a pair of 9 volt batteries. Produced in Korea around 1989-1991, it was never intended to be a high-quality serious instrument, although poor set-up, undressed frets, bad action, and a general lack of attention to detail have done it no favors so it is not altogether surprising that it has been referred to as the worst guitar ever.

SynthAxe

The SynthAxe is a guitar synthesizer system invented by Bill Aitken, built in Oxfordshire, UK, and first produced in 1986. Its idiosyncrasies include separate sets of strings for fretting and for triggering notes; a neck set at an obtuse angle to the body with evenly-spaced frets to facilitate playing higher up the neck; and a 6-key keyboard used to trigger notes as an alternative to the strings on the body. Such quirks of design are only possible because the SynthAxe is not an actual guitar but a guitar-like interface. Despite being used by Allan Holdsworth, Gary Moore and Al Di Meola, the SynthAxe was not a commercial success.

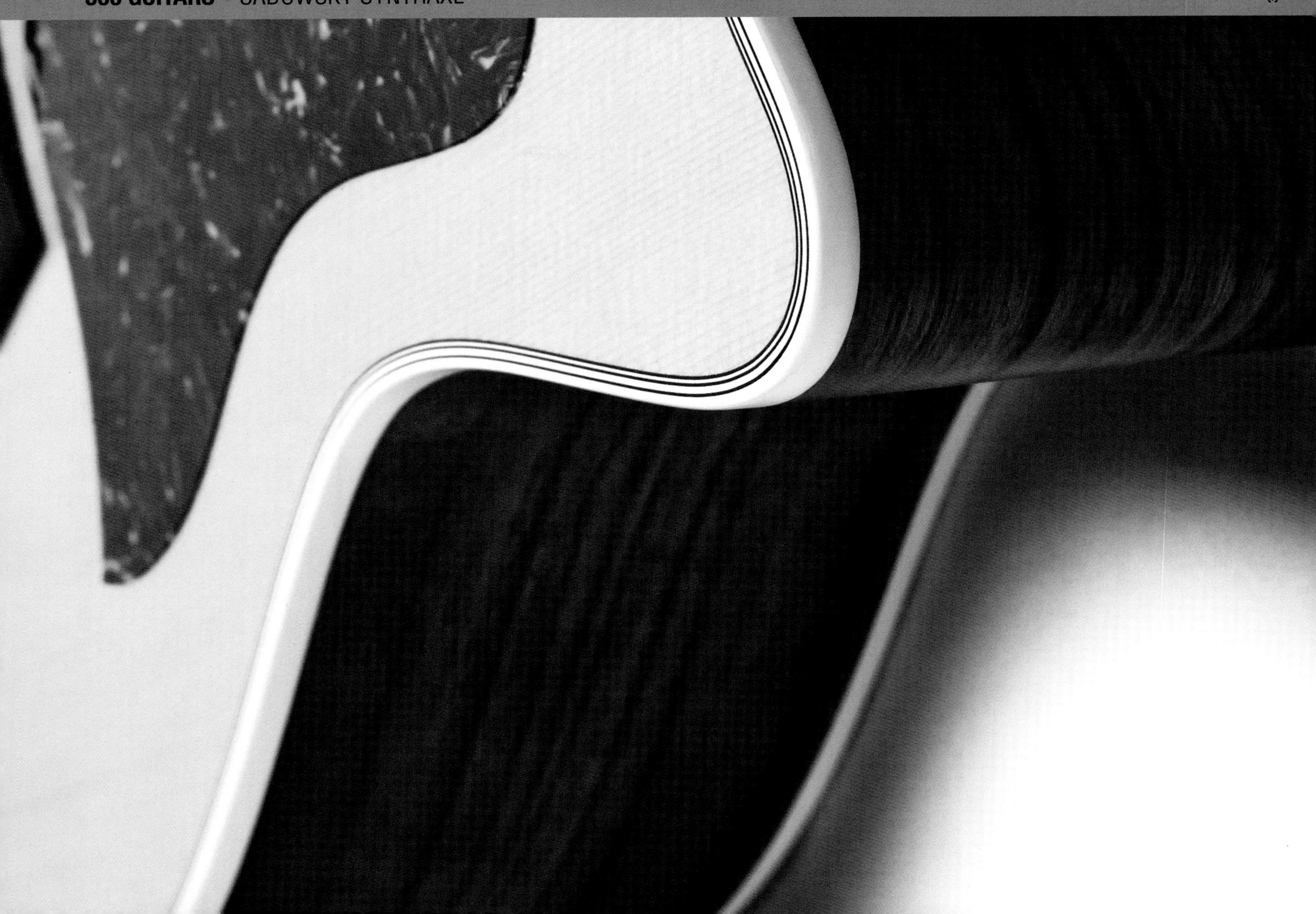

Takamine EN20 Jumbo

The Takamine EN20, first produced in 1986, has a jumbo body with no cutaway. It has a mahogany back and sides with a solid cedar top and a rosewood fingerboard without inlays. It is bound in black and white purfling and has gold hardware. It is a high-quality acoustic guitar with a "no frills" understated design. The large body produces a deep resonance while the high-grade timbers employed in the construction allow the notes to ring out with a clear and long sustain. Notable players include Pete Townshend.

Takamine Flying A

The Takamine Flying A is an acoustic guitar based on the design of a Gibson Flying V but with a more rounded, almost inflated-looking shape. Originally produced in 1983 and made in Japan, the guitar has rosewood back and sides with a bookmatched spruce top and a mahogany neck with 20-fret rosewood fingerboard and rosewood headstock overlay. The bridge is fitted with an undersaddle piezo pickup with controls on the upper rim for gain, bass and treble. The guitar's shape allows unhindered access to the higher frets for those that like to play up the neck.

Taylor "Baby Taylor"

The Baby Taylor is a dreadnought acoustic intended as a portable travel-friendly guitar. The back and sides are constructed from laminate and the top is Sitka spruce. The neck is Tropical American mahogany and has a 19-fret ebony fingerboard with 14 frets clear of the body and inlaid with pearloid dots. The bridge is of ebony while the headstock has a lexan overlay, tusq nut and enclosed diecast tuners. The body and neck are unbound while the soundhole rosette is laser-etched. The Baby has a sweet, full voice and great tone, and may be played using alternate tunings or high-strung.

Taylor Grand Auditorium

The Grand Auditorium is a body shape that has been applied to a number of acoustic guitars within Taylor's catalogue. Unveiled in 1994 on the occasion of Taylor's 20th Anniversary, it was the first body shape designed by company founder Bob Taylor. The guitar has the width of a dreadnaught but its narrower waist has the effect of making it appear smaller with the added benefit that the guitar is more comfortable to play while seated. Sonically it adds a treble accent to the tone and sharpens individual note definition. It is a versatile acoustic guitar for both fingerpicking and strumming style alike.

Taylor T5 Thinline

The Taylor T5 is a hybrid electric/acoustic guitar. It is of hollowbody construction and features an active soundboard with a compound radius. The neck uses Taylor's T-Lock neck joint system to precisely set the neck angle. The T5 is capable of authentic acoustic and full-on electric sounds, produced from a lipstick-sized humbucker at the bridge, a hidden neck humbucker, and a body sensor which reads the movement of the top and adds warmth to the acoustic tone. The T5 uses the Taylor Expression System and has a 5-way pickup selector, volume and two active pre-amp/EQ tone controls.

Teisco K-56

Teisco guitars were available in the West from 1964 to 1969. Aside from their own name, Teisco guitars appeared under many different brand names in Europe and the US. The K-56 is a distinctive-looking double-cutaway electric guitar produced in Japan from 1967. The top features a German carve and has Teisco's trademark striped pickguard in brushed aluminium mounted with three pickups, each with on/off switches, and master volume and tone controls. The guitar has a top-mounted tremolo behind the bridge, and the 22-fret neck has a rosewood fingerboard and a headstock with a 4+2 tuner layout.

Teisco May Queen

The Teisco May Queen is reminiscent of Vox's Teardrop, or perhaps more accurately the Vox Mando-Guitar, with an oval body shape featuring a lower cutaway so that it looks something like an artist's palette. The guitar is of semi-hollow construction and has a single f-hole, a pair of pickups with master volume, tone and 3-position pickup selector, an adjustable bridge and a Bigsby-like vibrato. The neck has a 22-fret fingerboard with dot markers. The Apollo-branded May Queen was a more up-market version and had two mini-humbuckers, binding on the neck and headstock, and pearloid block markers. (see picture below)

"My first love was the sound of guitar."
- Boz Scaggs

Teisco TB-64

Introduced in 1964, the TB-64 is Teisco's take on the Fender Bass VI. Although they have very similar body outlines, three pickups and a tremolo, nobody would ever confuse the two. The TB-64's three singlecoil pickups have three rocker on/off switches mounted above the neck pickup. The body features a cut-out monkey grip in the upper bout, a long time before Ibanez employed a similar concept in their JEM series guitars. The fingerboard has block position markers on the bass side of the neck, with the exception of the 12th fret, which has markers on both sides, and an oversized headstock with a 4+2 tuner arrangement.

Teuffel Birdfish

Ulrich Teuffel apprenticed in metalwork and construction at Mercedes-Benz and being inspired by the guitars of Steve Klein founded his own guitar company in 1988. The Birdfish is probably his most radical design and at first glance bears little resemblance to a guitar. A modular design, it does not seem to have a body as such. Pickups that seem to float in mid air actually sit on a rail beneath two tone bars. The guitar comes with five interchangeable pickups that may be used in any combination with up to three on the guitar together. The Birdfish also has MIDI capability.

Thomas Maltese Cross

The Maltese Surfer and the deluxe Maltese Falcon were built by Harvey Thomas, a luthier based in Midway, Washington. Thomas built all manner of crazy guitars and specialized in double and triplenecks. Both of the Maltese guitars have the Maltese Cross body shape, but the Falcon can be distinguished by its hook-shaped headstock. The hardware was bought from Germany, and pickguards were made out of perspex, with glitter having been liberally applied to the underside on the Falcon model. Necks were maple and were glued in, which seemed to make the guitars look more fragile. Notable users include Ian Hunter of Mott The Hoople. (see picture right)

Tokai Talbo

Tokai Guitars of Japan was founded in 1947 and is possibly best known for its high-quality replicas of Fender and Gibson guitars in the late 1970s and 1980s, which was a cause for concern to both those US companies. The Talbo, however, is an original design featuring an aluminium body. (The name Talbo is an abbreviation of Tokai Aluminium Body). The guitar features two Blazing Fire pickups, a hardtail bridge and a maple neck. There was also a Talbo bass, which featured a circular pickup. Recent years have seen variations such as the Talbo travel guitar with built-in speaker and the wooden-bodied Talbo Woody (surely an oxymoron).

Tonika Soviet-made Bass

The first generation of Tonika guitars and basses was made at the Lunacharsky factory of folk instruments in Leningrad (now Saint Petersburg). Built in the late 1960s, they were the first Soviet mass-produced guitars and basses. The next generation of guitars and basses was produced at Rostov, Ordjonikidze and Sverdlovsk. The shape is unusual and can only really be described as "lumpy". However, it does have a long upper horn and ought to balance nicely on a strap. However, they do not have a reputation for playability or sound.

Rick Toone Orchid Bass

Luthier Rick Toone of Milford, New Jersey, was commissioned to build a bass for Halie, a young female bass student. She had been finding it a struggle to fret notes in the lower register on a 34" scale bass, so a 32" scale was decided upon. To compensate for less string tension, Toone decided a stiffer neck was called for and ended up designing a trapezoidal neck profile, which provides great fretting leverage. The bass is sculpted in curly maple and swamp ash and is balanced for standing or seated performance, and also has good right arm support. Hardware includes Hipshot Ultralite tuners, and an EMG pickup with coil tap. (see pictures below and right)

Traben Bootsy Collins Star Bass

The Traben Bass Company is based in Clearwater, Florida, and was founded by Tracy Hoeft and Ben Chafin. Traben has created two signature basses for funk legend Bootsy Collins: the Bootzilla and the Star Bass. The Star Bass is based on the original Space Bass built in 1976 for Bootsy by a young luthier named Larry Pless. Aside from its star-shaped basswood body, the Traben Star Bass features a combination mirrored pickguard and bridge, five Rockfield J-type pickups, three Aguilar Amplification pre-amps for endless tone settings, a set-neck with rosewood fingerboard inlaid with shooting stars, and a star-shaped headstock.

Traben Phoenix Bass

The Traben Phoenix Bass has a basswood body with a quilted maple top and Traben's phoenix flame Bigger Bridge, designed to transmit more string energy to the top thereby creating more sustain. The bolt-on neck has a rosewood fingerboard with phoenix flame inlay. Pickups are Traben's own, one humbucker and one J-style, while electronics include a Traben T3 active pre-amp, 3-band EQ with volume and blend. The bass is available in both 34" scale 4-string and 35" scale 5-string versions.

Traveler Pro Series

The Traveler Pro Series guitar is the original Traveler model launched in 1992, and is still as popular. It is a small-bodied, headless guitar built from Eastern American hard maple with a 22-fret rosewood fingerboard and tuners mounted in the body itself. Pickups are a magnetic singlecoil plus a Shadow piezo pickup under the bridge saddle for acoustic sound, with a volume for each and a selector switch on the detachable leg rest. For private practice, the player can listen via a pair of stethophones, which connect to a diaphragm mounted beneath the bridge - absolutely no electricity is required, this is acoustic personal monitoring.

Travis Bean TB1000A

Travis Bean began production of his metal-neck guitars back in 1974 with original designs such as the TB1000A or Artist model. With a shape not unlike Gibson's 335, the body is made out of koa and has a carved top. The aluminium neck has an open T in the headstock and is set deep inside the body, under the pickups and bridge. At the hardtail bridge the strings pass through the aluminium center section of the body for increased sustain. The guitar also has two alnico humbucking pickups with volume and tone for each, and a rosewood fingerboard with block inlay position markers.

Travis Bean 2000 Bass

The TB2000 is a classic Travis Bean bass dating back to 1974. Like the guitars, it has a body made of koa and an aluminium neck and center body section running beneath the pickups and bridge. The use of aluminium was supposed to eradicate truss rod adjustments, warped necks and expanding/contracting neck issues. The two pickups are mounted straight into the aluminium center block and the tone is said to be incredible, with sustain that goes on forever. Notable players include Bill Wyman, who had four custom-order short-scale TB2000s made for him. A fretless model was also available.

James Trussart Steelcaster Bass

James Trussart, based in Los Angeles, builds guitars and basses with hollow bodies made of steel. Designed to look and feel like vintage instruments, they will often feature a rusted finish. Some feature artwork or engravings while others might have an alligator finish, which involves the body being wrapped in alligator skin, immersed in water and allowed to corrode for a few weeks. The Steelcaster Bass is loosely styled after the Fender Precision and has P and J pickups on a "holey" body of perforated steel, which reduces weight and eliminates feedback. The tone is said to be fat and resonant with an edge that cuts through.

James Trussart Steeldeville

The Steel Deville is a 24" scale guitar of a familiar singlecut design with a hollow steel body and a bolt-on maple neck. The 10" radius rosewood fingerboard has 24 medium jumbo frets and the headstock features a recessed steel head cap. Pickups are a choice of Trussart, Seymour Duncan or TV Jones and are controlled via two volumes, two tones and a 3-way pickup selector. The bridge is a tune-o-matic with a Bigsby vibrato available as an option. The steel body is available in a variety of rusty, antique and shiny finishes with optional engravings and perforations.

Rick Turner Model One

Rick Turner's Model One guitar employs a graphite neck for increased stability and sustain, and a cylindrical arch to decrease the standing waves created by parallel surfaces. It is a solid-bodied electric guitar with the aesthetics of a classical instrument. Its sound can range from detailed acoustic tones to screaming lead without breaking up or producing any unwanted feedback. The guitar features piezo pickups and Turner's own hand-wound humbucker mounted on a rotating plate in the faux soundhole. A pickup blender control and an EQ frequency sweeper give access to an astonishing array of tones. Notable players include Lindsey Buckingham.

Rick Turner Renaissance Bass

Rick Turner's Renaissance Bass is an elegant instrument built from quality tonewoods and with an uncluttered appearance. The hollowbody is walnut with a cedar or walnut top and without any soundholes. The one-piece maple neck is available in 34" or 35" scale length, 4 or 5-string, and fretted or fretless options. The Renaissance is powered by a Turner-designed piezo pickup and Highlander pre-amp, and is said to have almost unlimited tonal possibilities from jazz to rock to bluegrass. The sound produced is articulate and has an organic vibe to it with a natural decay so that it could be said to breathe.

Univox Eagle Bass

The Univox Eagle Bass was built in Japan, circa 1977, and is based on the Fender Precision Bass. The body is made from solid walnut and the top has been elaborately carved with an eagle design. All the other features - bolt-on maple neck, pickups, etc - are standard P-Bass fare. The bass was built in Japan's Matsumoku factory where Univox, Aria, Washburn, Westone and many other brands were also produced. There was also a similarly finished Strat-type guitar produced as well as Strats with two different dragon designs made for the Aria Pro II brand.

Vashon Guitars "Green"

Vashon Guitars is headquartered on Vashon Island, Washington, and was founded by Bob Krinsky in 2006 to fill a void in the archtop electric guitar market where only the very wealthiest players could obtain superbly crafted premium electric archtop, acoustic and jazz box guitars. The Vashon Green is an archtop cutaway built from maple with a 24.6" scale length and a rosewood fingerboard inlaid with pearloid block markers. Two humbuckers are controlled via a volume and tone for each and a 3-way pickup selector. In keeping with its name the guitar is finished in a luscious green.

Veleno Original

The Veleno Original is an electric guitar machined from two solid billets of aircraft-grade aluminium. The 24-fret aluminium neck, guaranteed never to warp, is fretted to within 1/1000 of an inch. It features coil tappable twin humbuckers with volume and tone for each, plus pickup selector and high-low tone switch. Designed and built by John Veleno in the early 1970s, the goal was to build a great sounding guitar that was easy to play. That he chose aluminium as his medium meant that the guitar looked highly original too, with examples produced in gold plating, chrome and anodized finishes and each with a real ruby inset in the headstock.

Vigier Excalibur Surfreter Fretless Guitar

Vigier Guitars of Grigny, France, was founded in 1978 by Patrice Vigier and is known for design innovations such as fretless Delta Metal fingerboards made from a brass alloy. The Excalibur Surfreter has a solid two-piece body with a top of flamed maple and a bolt-on maple neck, three DiMarzio pickups (two humbuckers and a center singlecoil), and a fixed bridge. The Delta Metal fretless fingerboard makes the guitar sound amazing. It has incredible sustain while slides, slurs and vibrato can all be produced from the fingers. It even sustains well on the unwound strings, and can be used for authentic-sounding slide guitar without the slide! (see picture right and the Excalibur Custom guitar on p354)

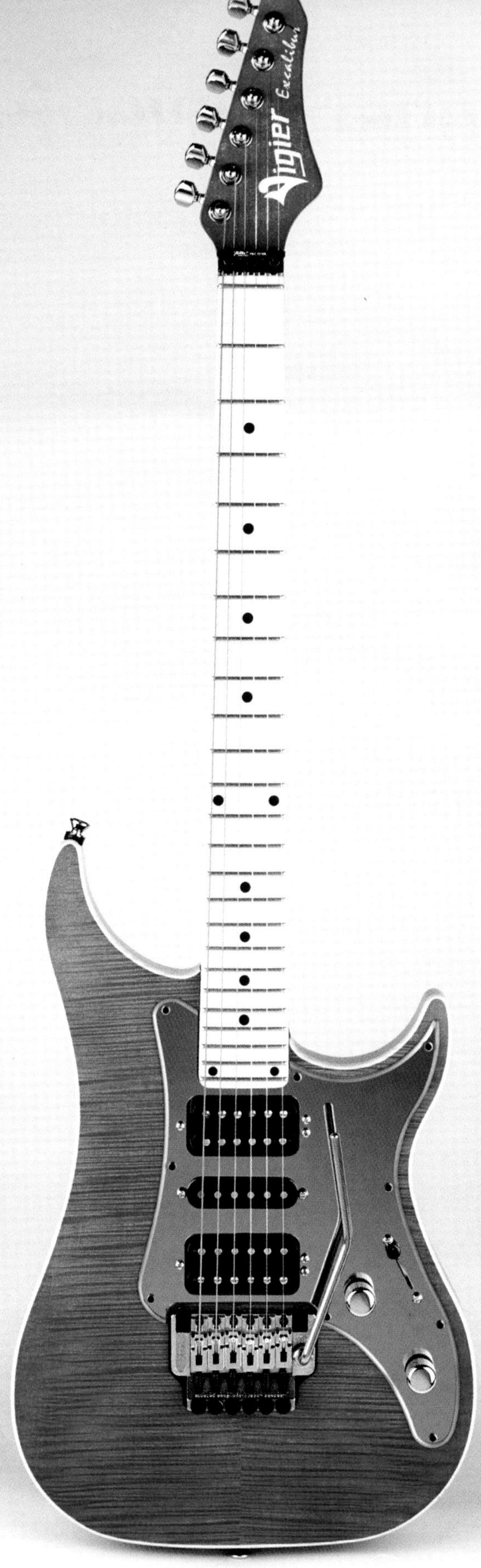
Vigier
Excalibur

Vigier Roger Glover Bass

The Roger Glover Custom Bass has a 2-piece body with flamed maple top and bolt-on maple neck. The neck uses Vigier's 10/90 Neck System (10% carbon and 90% maple) in which the neck has a dense carbon strip replacing the more traditional truss rod and which eradicates loss of sustain while remaining solid. The fingerboard is rosewood and has 24 medium frets and is inlaid with phosphorescent dots. The bass is fitted with two singlecoils with an active hum-cancelling circuit, and with controls for volume, balance, bass, medium and treble. (see a Vigier guitar opposite)

Vline Sword Guitar

The Vline "La Péniche" (The Sword) is a headless guitar shaped like a sword, with a body made from resin and hardware fashioned from brass. It was built in the early 1980s in Chalais, France, by avant garde luthier Vincent Breton. Breton had been a protégé of fellow Frenchman and luthier James Trussart, and would spend months at a time building a single guitar, making even the smallest parts by hand. Pickups too were handmade and would be hidden out of sight in the guitar body. Breton died in the mid 1990s and it is believed that he built approximately 20 guitars in his lifetime.

Alexandre Voboam, 5-Double-Course Guitar, 1670

The National Music Museum at the University of South Dakota, Vermillion, has in its collection a baroque guitar made by Alexandre Voboam in 1670. The guitar has five double courses and ten gut frets, which are tied on. The body length is 35" with a scale length of 25". It features an intricate three-dimensional "wedding cake" rose inside the guitar's soundhole, which is surrounded by inlays of ebony and ivory echoing the binding around the body's edge. The back is French juniper and has inlaid stringing of ebony and ivory, while the back of the neck and headstock are veneered ebony with ivory stringing.

Rene Voboam Baroque Guitar, 1641

An earlier baroque guitar from 1641 by René Voboam is in Oxford's Ashmolean Museum. It features a flat back of five ribs in yew, inlaid with ebony and holly stringing. The sides are in ebony with two inlaid holly panel lines. Neck, headstock and fingerboard are ebony veneered, with the neck featuring a leaf-trail design, and the ten tuning pegs being made of ebony. The soundhole is inset with a delicate 5-tier parchment rosette in a Star of David design. The scale length is 26" but the whole instrument is shorter than modern-day guitars because of the position of the bridge.

Vox Mando Guitar

The Mando Guitar is essentially a short-scale 12-string guitar. Its tuning is equivalent of putting a capo on the 12th fret of a regular 12-string guitar. The guitar has an "artist's palette" body shape (which probably inspired Teisco's May Queen), two singlecoil pickups, with volume, tone and pickup selector switch. The guitar enabled guitarists to easily obtain a mandolin-like sound and pitch while retaining a familiar tuning. Notable players include George Harrison who played a Vox Mando on The Beatles' "Words of Love".

Vox Mark III

Vox, already known for their amplifiers, catapulted onto the guitar scene in 1962 with the creation of the Vox Phantom, a pentagonal guitar. The Mark III follows this tradition of unusual shapes with a teardrop body sculpted from aspen. A favorite of Brian Jones, Vox withdrew production of all its guitars in the 1970s but reissued USA-manufactured guitars for a while in the late 1990s.

Vox Guitar Organ

The Vox Guitar Organ, which first appeared in 1966, was based on the Phantom design with the guts of a Vox miniaturized transistor organ inside the body. Split frets wired into the organ circuitry are activated when contact is made by a fretted string and thus the relevant note is produced. However, with so much circuitry inside the guitar the body was basically hollow with a pickguard mounted on top, and so the guitar's natural tone suffered. Additionally, the organ circuitry was notoriously unreliable and so this revolutionary instrument never caught on. (see picture right)

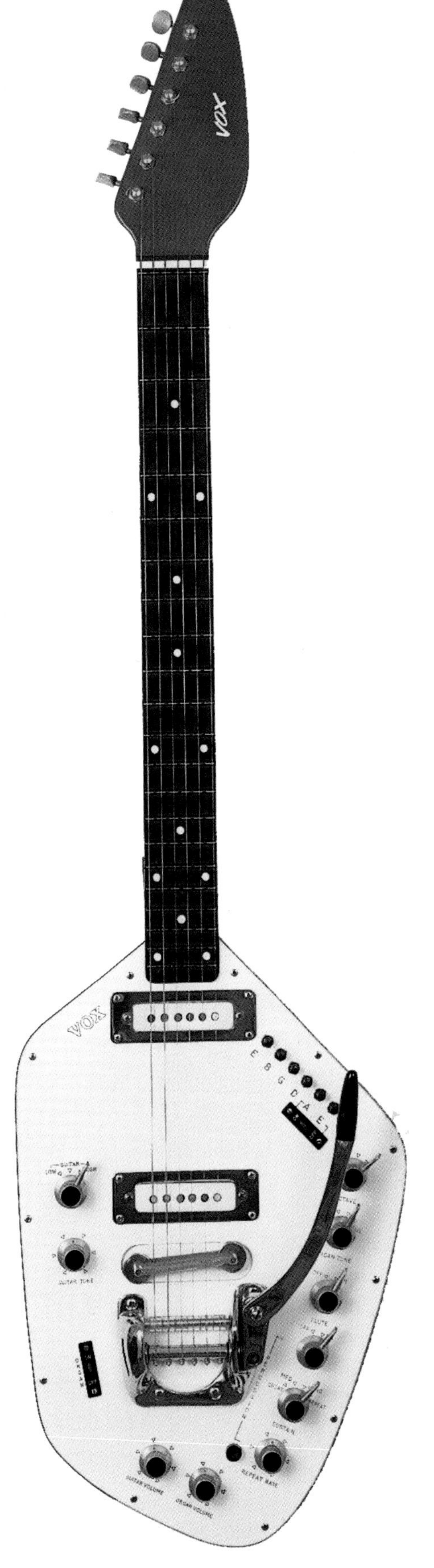

Vox Virage DC

The Virage DC is one of Vox's modern professional-quality guitars. It is contoured using 3-dimensional carving techniques for balance and playability. The hand-carved neck joint has an inverse heel for better access to the higher frets and the neck is set using a long tenon joint, which provides a greater contact area. The body is carved internally with a pair of integral tonebars where semi-hollow guitars have a center block. This combines the resonance of a hollowbody with the attack of a solidbody. Two pickups ombine characteristics of P90, humbucker and singlecoils, while a simple switching system makes choosing tones easy.

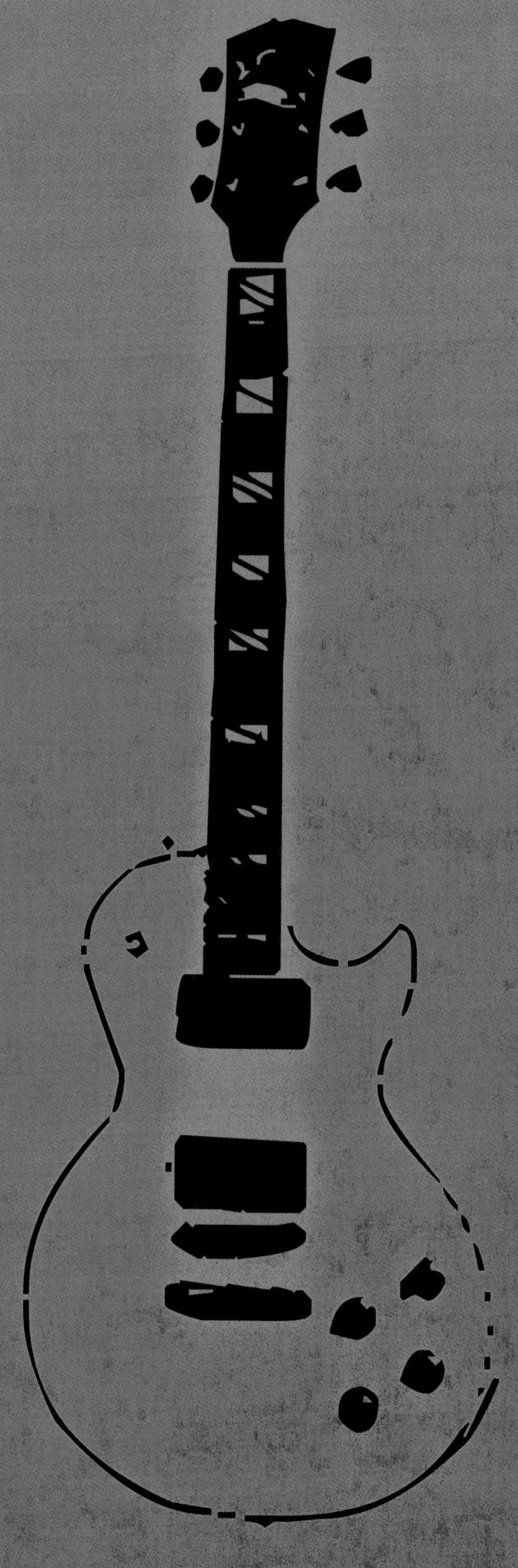

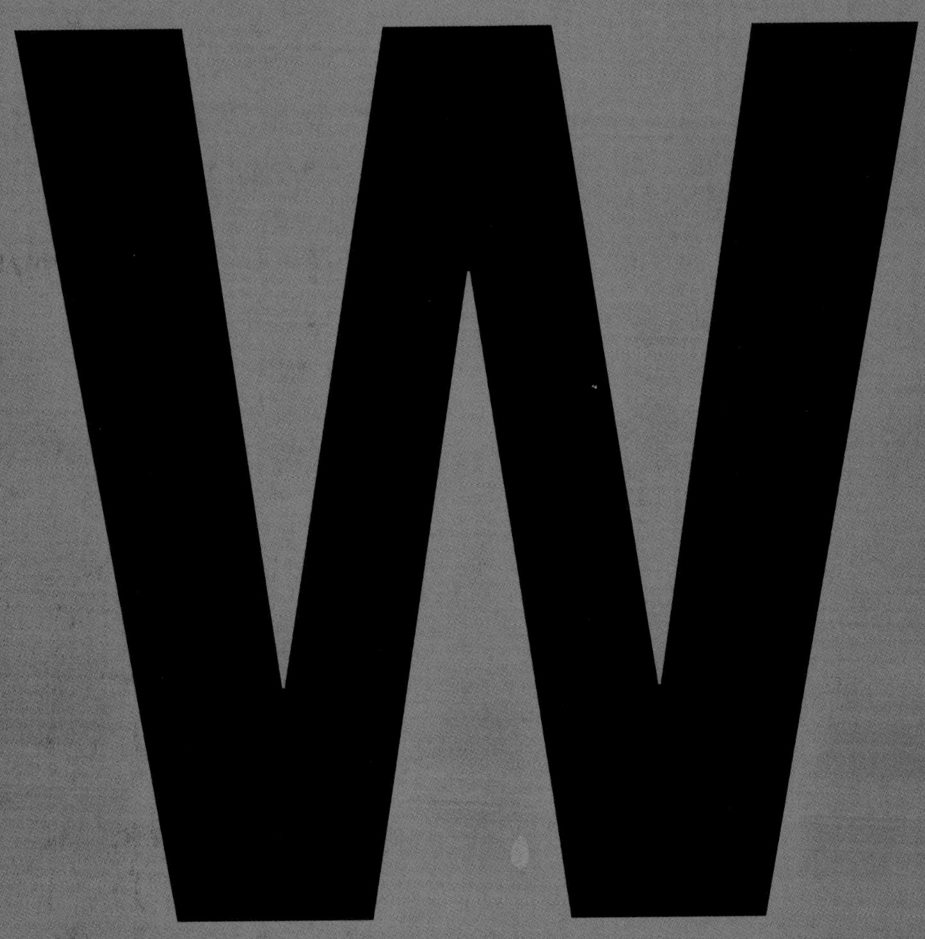

Wal Custom Mark I Fretless Bass

Wal was founded in 1984 by Ian Waller and Pete Smith and produced handmade basses in the "Electric Wood" shop in High Wycombe, Buckinghamshire, UK. They were quality instruments, typically featuring exotic woods and custom electronics. The Custom Series first appeared in 1983 and had bodies constructed of a mahogany core sandwiched between laminates of timbers such as American walnut, schedua/hydua, padauk and wenge. Each pickup actually contains two individual pickups per string, wired into humbucking mode, and is essential to the unique Wal sound. Mick Karn of Japan played two fretless Mark I basses, one with African tulipwood facings, the other a cherry solidbody. (see picture below)

Wandre Rock 6

Wandre Guitars were designed by Wandré Pioli (1926-2004) and built in his factory in Cavriago, Italy, from 1959 to 1969. The Rock 6 is a typically eccentric Wandre guitar. The sculpted mahogany body features a large heart-shaped hole behind the tailpiece and a smaller round hole near the treble-side horn. The guitar has an aluminium neck backed with polystyrene plastic coating. The aluminium rod forming the neck continues down the front of the body and terminates at the W tailpiece. The bridge and two Davoli pickups are attached to this rod, which is in turn bolted to the body. Volume and tone controls are housed on what looks like a left-over metal pickup cover. (see picture below)

Wandre Spazial 608

The Wandre Spazial is more conventional looking than some of the brand's models with a curvy body shape with rounded contours and edges. It has the usual neck formed from an aluminium rod with a fingerboard attached at the front and molded polystyrene on the back. The headstock varies between two types: aluminium slotted with wooden center section, or a big plate of aluminium with tuners attached. The 20-fret fingerboard has colored Wandre position markers and the two Davioli pickups (built by Wandré Pioli's friend and collaborator Athos Davioli) sit on an oddly-shaped plastic pickguard. These guitars were often finished in a two-color blow-dry-burst.

Washburn

Warr Guitars

Warr Guitars, like the Chapman Stick and the Mobius Megatar, are designed to be played touch-style, and are available in eight, ten and twelve string models in a number of different styles to suit tappers of all tastes. The Metal Series has an aggressive BC Rich-inspired body shape and maple neck/fingerboard, while the Artisan Series is a semi-hollow touch instrument with floating Bartolini and piezo pickups, and the Phalanx Series has up to 14 strings with the bass side tuned to the same as a 6-string bass and the guitar side an octave above.

Warwick Buzzard Bass

Warwick Basses was founded in Germany in 1982 by Hans-Peter Wilfer. In 1985 he was approached by The Who's John Entwistle to create a bass for him and together they designed the Buzzard Bass. Visually it is a very odd design with an avian quality to it, especially the headstock that resembles a cruel hooked beak. The basic Buzzard model has a Zebranol body and a bolt-on ovangkol neck with a 24-fret wenge fingerboard. It also features active pickups with 2-band EQ. The John Entwistle signature edition is similar but is of through-neck construction.

Washburn AB40 Acoustic Bass

The Washburn AB40 is an acoustic-electric bass with an arched top [archtop?] body and a Venetian cutaway. The back and sides are made of maple and the top is of select spruce and features Washburn's patented soundslots in the place of the usual soundhole, which reduce the possibility of feedback. The neck has a rosewood fingerboard with dot markers and gold Grover diecast tuners. The bass has a custom piezo pickup in the rosewood bridge with controls mounted on the front of the body. (see picture on opposite page)

Washburn Nuno Bettencourt N4 Vintage

The N4 is a signature model of the Extreme guitarist Nuno Bettencourt. There are two N4 models: the N4 Vintage, with an aged alder body, and the N4SA, which has a swamp ash body. Both are double cutaway guitars featuring a Stevens extended cutaway 5-bolt neck joint allowing unrestricted access to the top frets on the ebony fingerboard. The necks on each are maple and have reverse-style 6-in-a-row headstocks with Grover tuners. Pickups are a Bill Lawrence L500 in the bridge position and a Seymour Duncan '59 at the neck, and controls are single volume and pickup selector. Both guitars have a 25" scale and an original Floyd Rose tremolo. (see picture below)

Washburn Paul Stanley PS1800

The PS1800 Paul Stanley Signature model has an asymmetric body shape with an extended lower horn, slightly reminiscent of the Ibanez Iceman that Stanley used to favor. The body and set-neck are mahogany with a rosewood 22-fret neck with mother of pearl/abalone split block inlays. The pickups are by Randall with a volume for each, master tone and a pickup selector. The guitar has a 24.75" scale and is installed with the Buzz Feiten Tuning System to ensure correct intonation across the whole neck. Grover tuners, a tune-o-matic bridge and a special Paul Stanley tailpiece add the finishing touches.

Washburn WB200S Baby Jumbo Acoustic

The WB200S acoustic guitar has the Baby Jumbo body style, which gives the appearance of a compressed Jumbo with an exaggerated inward curve at the waist and an oval soundhole. The back and sides are of mahogany with a solid spruce top and ivoroid binding on front and back. The mahogany neck has a bound rosewood fingerboard with 20 frets, joining the body at the 14th. Other features include a bound rosewood capped headstock with Grover tuners, rosewood bridge, Buzz Feiten Tuning System with Feiten nut and compensated saddle. (see picture below, and a range of Washburn guitars on p374)

WATKINS
RAPIER 44

Watkins Rapier 44

Watkins Electric Music was formed in 1949 in London by Charlie Watkins and his brother, Reg Watkins, but didn't release its first solid electric guitar until 1957. In 1966 they introduced the Rapier Series, designed by Reg Watkins. With offset double cutaways, Watkins Hi-Lo tremolo and a 6-in-a-line headstock it was reminiscent of the Fender Stratocaster. The Rapier 44 had four pickups and was the top-of-the-line model in a series designed as budget instruments. Its original retail price was £30. Watkins Rapiers still have their fans today and the sounds have been described as occasionally scratchy and bright with clear ringing chords. (see picture left)

Watkins Sapphire

The Watkins Sapphire was introduced in the mid 1960s and appeared under the WEM (Watkins Electric Music) brand and, after 1968, the Wilson brand. The later name change came about when the Watkins brothers wanted to market their guitars under a separate brand from their amps, and so chose their mother's maiden name. The Sapphire, like the Rapier, has a design based on the Strat and borrows the same Burns-like split pickguard as used on the Rapier Bass. Unlike the Rapier it dispenses with the Strat-like headstock and opts for a 3+3 style instead. A 12-string model was also available, and the 6-string came with a WEM/Wilson vibrato. (see picture on p380)

Wayne Guitars Hydra

Wayne Guitars was founded in the late 1990s by Wayne Charvel, formerly of Charvel Guitars, and are hand built by Wayne Charvel and his oldest son, Michael. The Hydra is an oddly shaped guitar. The outline of the body suggests it might have been based on the initials W.C., but Jerry Sewell, who worked for Charvel in 1977, designed the body shape. The guitar caught the eye of Eddie Van Halen who owns a yellow example with gold hardware.

Weissenborn Style 4

Hermann C. Weissenborn emigrated from Germany to the US in about 1902 and worked as a violin and piano maker in New York and later in Los Angeles. With the then-current popularity of Hawaiian music he began building ukuleles and guitars. Weissenborn developed a hollow-necked guitar specifically for Hawaiian or lap-steel playing. Generally, they have an hour-glass shape with gently sloping shoulders and a neck that is integral to the body. The Style 4 was the most luxuriously appointed with rope binding around the front, back, neck, headstock and soundhole. Such guitars were popular until the late 1920s when resonator guitars made their appearance.

Wendler electrocoustic

Wendler electrocoustic guitars have resonant, thinly carved bodies of Western red cedar, specially selected for tone, and hand-carved necks of mahogany or maple. Guitars feature Wendler's MagPi dual passive pickup system employing both humbucker and piezo pickups. Magnetic pickups are of the floating variety as used on archtop jazz guitars and do not require cavities in the body. Similarly, the electrics are beneath the pickguard with a volume control and bias control that blends between the humbucker and piezo. With no routing of the body for pickups and controls it is free to resonate in a more accurate acoustic manner. (see picture right)

"..I wanted to create music that was so different that my mother could tell me from anyone else"
- Les Paul

Westone The Rail Bass

Westone guitars and basses were popular in the 1980s when they provided high quality of manufacturing and value for money. They were built in the Matsumoku factory in Japan. The Rail Bass is one of many small-bodied headless basses that flooded the market in the wake of the revolutionary Steinberger. However, it isn't merely a clone; it has a neat trick of its own.
The body is divided into two sections connected only by two metal rails upon which a sliding pickup can be positioned anywhere between the two body sections giving instant access to different tones.

Wilcox SD-10 Pedal Steel

Wilcox Steel Guitars builds affordable pedal steels. The SD-10 is a singlenecked steel that has been built on a doubleneck frame with an arm pad where the first neck would normally be. It has three pedals, four knee levers, a 10-string aluminium neck and a Formica-covered body in a choice of marine blue or black. It also features Grover tuners, Jerry Wallace or George L. pickup and has adjustable chrome legs.

Wilkes Guitars The Answer

Doug Wilkes started building guitars in 1972 and by the 1980s, with a team of nine people in his Stoke-on-Trent workshop, Wilkes Guitars became the largest independent guitar factory in the UK. A number of innovative instruments were built such as a fretless bass with slap plates mounted on the fingerboard, and a semi-fretted, semi-fretless bass to allow players the best of both worlds. The Answer is another guitar with sliding pickups. The guitar has a single humbucker that splits into two halves, which can be moved independently on internal rails, giving access to singlecoil and humbucker sounds in different positions and allowing endless tone variations.

Williams Keytar V-2

Some would argue that the Williams Keytar isn't a guitar at all. But it does have strings and pickups, and it does sound like a guitar. The Keytar V2 is a guitar aimed at keyboard players who, perhaps in a band situation, might be required to double on guitar. It is a large triangular instrument, designed to be played on a strap, with a 2-octave keyboard, 24 strings and two EMG pickups. The left hand plays the keyboard while the right hand strums or plucks the strings. It has a clavinet-like mechanism using rubber pads which, when depressed, fret the otherwise damped strings.

Wilson Brothers The Ventures

The instrumental rock band The Ventures were famous endorsees of the Mosrite Ventures model guitar through 1963-1968. When not contracted to Mosrite they usually played Fender guitars and basses. The Wilson Brothers Ventures guitars is a range of instruments designed with specifications from The Ventures themselves, and based on Mosrite and Fender guitars. The VM-65, for example, is distinctly Mosrite-inspired and has an agathis top with German carve, and a bolt-on maple neck with 22-fret rosewood fingerboard. It has two APS-9 (P90-like) pickups, with the neck position pickup slanted as on a Mosrite. The tremolo is Strat-like instead of the top-mounted Bigsby-type vibrato.

"The Strat covers the complete spectrum of human emotion...the tremolo enables you to do anything - you can hit any note known to mankind "- Jeff Beck

Washburn
Washburn

Washburn
N4
Washburn

Wilson SAB Semi Bass

Watkins Electric Music built the Wilson SAB Semi-Bass in the UK. The SAB is a short-scale bass and was a sibling to the SAF and SAT guitar models introduced in 1969. It is a double cutaway archtop with two f-holes and finished in sunburst polyester with a mother of pearl crown device inset in the headstock. The neck is a 2-ply laminate of sycamore (European maple) and has a mahogany neck with 24 frets. The bass features Schaller pickups and tuners, and has a master volume, individual tone controls for each pickup, and a pickup selector switch. (see picture below)

Wilson Ranger

The Wilson Ranger was available with one or two pickups, with the single pickup model having the pickup in the neck position. The Ranger 1 and 2 models were launched in 1968 and were aimed at the entry-level guitarist. They have a certain retro charm to their asymmetrical non-cutaway futuristic styling. The Ranger is a solidbodied guitar with a mahogany neck with a 22-fret rosewood fingerboard, single coil pickups, volume and tone controls, and an intoned bridge adjustable for height only. The only compromise on the usual Wilson quality seems to be the basic open-backed tuners. (see picture below)

Wishbass Peanut

Wishbasses are built by Steve Wishnevsky of Winston Salem, North Carolina, specializing in highly individual ergonomically-carved fretless basses with a rustic quality to them. They have the minimum amount of electronics (just a volume control between the pickup and output) and a basic wooden bridge. The Peanut Bass is the most popular model and has a walnut through-neck body with a jatoba fingerboard. The bass has an extra deep lower cutaway to allow access to the top of the fingerboard, which extends nearly all the way to the single J-type pickup in the bridge position. (see picture left)

Woody B's Internal Combustion Guitar V8

The Internal Combustion Guitar is designed to recreate the effect of playing in front of a bank of Marshall amps and finding that "sweet spot", which enables some blistering guitar playing to happen, but without the extreme volume and need for a bank of Marshalls. The guitar has a "driver pickup" mounted near the bridge. The signal from this is fed out to a small low-wattage amp and then back into the guitar, which has an acoustic resonance chamber with built-in speaker that brings the guitar to life with resonance and sustain. A Lace Alumitone neck pickup captures the resulting sound and sends it through to the main amp.

Wurlitzer Wild One Gemini Stereo Guitar

Wurlitzer, known for their organs, was a brand that appeared briefly on guitars made in the Holman-Woodell guitar factory in Neodesha, Kansas (which also built the short-run of LaBaye 2x4 guitars). First appearing in late 1965 as part of the Wild One range alongside the Cougar and the Wildcat, the Gemini has an angular double-cutaway design. It has two Sensitone pickups each with a Jazz/Rock switch that selects between different capacitors. Other controls were two volumes, two tones, a fader for stereo effects and a 3-way pickup selector. Wurlitzer guitars suffered from poor finishes with many being returned to the factory, and in 1967 were no longer being produced by Holman-Woodell.

Wilson

No. 051 Limited Edition
DiMarzio
design by peter solomon

XOX Audio Tools The Handle

The Handle is a beautifully sculpted cutting-edge guitar designed in Italy by Peter Solomon. It has a mono-chassis, hollow-sectioned, carbon fiber construction providing lossless transmission of acoustic vibrations, while making it environmentally friendly and very light at only 4.4 lbs. It also makes it virtually indestructible and extremely rigid, and will stay in tune despite temperature fluctuations. The slim body has an ergonomic concave back and a cut-out design giving it its name, plus a super slim neck for ease of playing up to the top fret. Other features include a Hipshot bridge, GraphTech nut and DiMarzio pickups.

Yamaha BB714BS Billy Sheehan Signature Bass

Sheehan built his technique on his 'Franken-Fender' P-Bass, but in 1985 he joined forces with Yamaha to create a unique guitar which reflects his style. Unusual ceramic pickup magnets give the bass an aggressive feel, while the humbucker in the neck position warms up the tone slightly. Using ferrous blades instead of usual pole pieces avoids drop outs when bending strings to emulate Billy's style.

Yamaha EZ-EG

The EZ-EG is a digital guitar intended for home use, primarily as a teaching instrument. It has 12 fret buttons for each string on the fingerboard, and notes are triggered by plucking or strumming six plastic bars in the place of strings on the body. It has 20 internal sounds and a small selection of tunes that the beginner can play along with; the "fretboard" lights up to show where to play! It is not of sufficient build-quality to withstand life as a stage instrument but for the recording guitarist it can be used as a MIDI controller with access to all manner of synthesizer sounds.

"When you strum a guitar you have everything - rhythm, bass, lead and melody."
- David Gilmore

Yamaha Pacifica

The Yamaha Pacifica 112 has been a best-selling guitar since its introduction in 1993. Although an entry-level guitar, quality and build-construction have not been sacrificed. The Pacifica 112 has a solid alder body, maple neck with rosewood fingerboard, plus solid reliable hardware and a humbucker and two singlecoil pickups. Other manufacturers that had been using laminated bodies on their budget-priced guitars needed a serious re-think after the Pacifica showed them how it should be done. It is a fantastic first guitar for the beginner, more than able to hold its own on stage, and - for those who love to tinker - is easily upgradable.

Yamaha SG2000

In 1976 Yamaha sought to create a classic guitar that could compete with the best. The SG2000 (known as the SBG2000 in the US to avoid confusion with a certain other guitar) was launched and, with some refinements suggested by Carlos Santana, went on to become the so-called "Les Paul Killer". The guitar is of neck-through-body construction, made from maple and mahogany, with a carved maple top, and a 22-fret ebony fingerboard. The tune-o-matic bridge has a brass sustain plate beneath it, while two alnico humbuckers, Gotoh tuners and gold hardware put the finishing touches to an incredible instrument.

Yamaha SB-1C Bass

Yamaha first started producing steel string and electric guitars in 1966 and some of their earlier instruments can only be described as eccentric-looking. The SB-1C was released in 1968 and available until 1971. The body is kidney-shaped with cutaways and it has forearm contouring around the top edge. It is a bolt-on neck instrument with a scale length of just under 30" and has a single pickup in the neck position; one could imagine that the tone would be quite boomy. The bass is finished in bold solid blue, yellow or red.

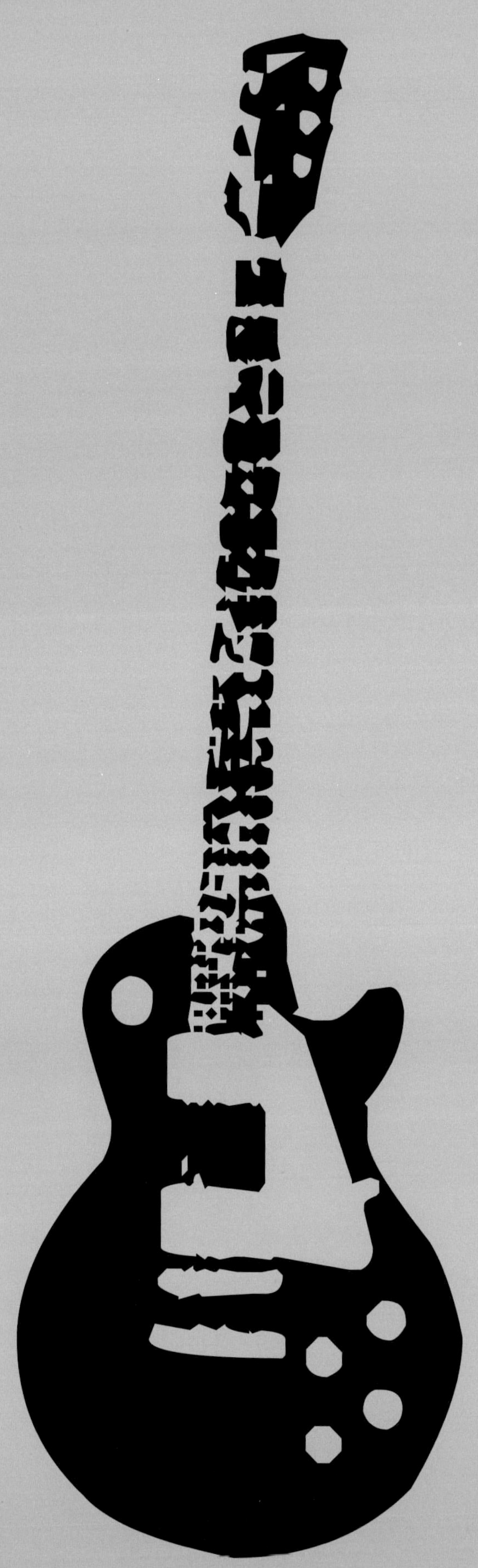

Zachary Guitars "IKEA"

Zachary Guitars are handcrafted in Canada by Alex Csiky. One of his more intriguing instruments is the IKEA guitar. It has a body built from multi-piece knotty pine, which is actually from an unfinished end table bought from IKEA for $15. The guitar has a singlecut body similar to that of a Danelectro 56'U2 and is fitted with a pair of P90 humbuckers. The neck is a single piece of mahogany with a 24-fret rosewood fingerboard. For an encore Csiky went on to build the Butcher Block Tele, with a body made out of an IKEA solid birch chopping board.

Zemaitis GZMF501 NT

Tony Zemaitis (1935-2002) was a legendary British luthier of Lithuanian descent, known for his metal and pearl-fronted guitars and basses as used by the likes of Ronnie Wood, Ronnie Lane and Eric Clapton. His guitars often featured metal parts with artistic engravings by Danny O'Brien. Since Zemaitis' death in 2002, the guitars have been produced in Japan under the watchful eye of Tony Zemaitis, Jr. The GZMF501 NT is a singlecut mahogany-bodied guitar with one-piece mahogany neck and 24-fret ebony fingerboard. Pickups are two DiMarzio PAF types and the guitar has a duralumin Zemaitis bridge and tailpiece and a duralumin top engraved by Danny O'Brien.

Zemaitis PF3005 Classic Pearl Front

The first pearl-front guitar was made for the Rolling Stones' Ronnie Wood while he was still in The Faces. The Zemaitis PF3005 is a guitar in the same tradition. It has a mahogany neck with a rosewood fingerboard, crafted onto a stunning mahogany body inlayed with an abalone mosaic. The guitar also has three DiMarzio Custom Stack pickups and engraved duralumin metal hardware. Zemaitis is known for creating precision instruments, but any technical skills are totally eclipsed by the beauty of the finished guitars. (see picture right and another member of the Zemaitis family on p395)

Zerberus Hydra

Zerberus Guitars, based in Germany, was formed in 2002 and aims to provide the modern guitarist with high-performance guitars that are aesthetically pleasing. The Hydra has a double cutaway design with plenty of access up to the 24th fret. The body is sculpted from korina with a bookmatched maple veneer archtop, and the neck is of maple with rosewood fingerboard. The Hydra has great natural attack and sustain and its two humbuckers are selected via a 5-position switch with two coil-tap options giving a wealth of tonal options. The guitar also features the Q-Deluxe Floyd Rose licensed tremolo, and is hand-built in Korea to Zerberus' specifications.

Zoybar Open Source Guitar

Zoybar is a modular hardware platform for creating custom electric string instruments with integrated effects, inspired by the open source movement within the world of computing. Put simply, it is a modular guitar system. As Zoybar founder and designer Ziv Bar Ilan says, "The Zoybar components provide research and development tools as a sustainable, playable prototype platform. The same modular parts can be assembled as different instruments, can be changed during the performance and also be mounted with numerous special effects, just by adding and changing their position across the profile grooves." Translated, it's a Meccano for guitarists!

ACKNOWLEDGMENTS

The publishers would like to thank the following picture libraries for their kind permission to use their images:

Getty (Redferns Collection): 12, 17, 24, 29, 36, 51, 52, 53, 62, 65, 75, 109, 111, 112, 113, 118, 119,123, 136, 137, 150, 151,160, 164, 166, 167, 170, 174, 177, 179, 181, 183, 188, 190, 193, 196, 206, 207, 209, 213, 219, 241, 254, 256, 263, 264, 274, 275, 277, 282, 289, 294, 298, 303, 305,317,321, 324, 327 328, 336, 341, 350, 354, 356, 363.

Istockphoto: 132, 134, 138, 155, 168, 217, 242, 277, 301, 307, 310, 331, 345.

Balafon Image Bank (managed by Jawbone Press): 23, 46, 72, 84, 89, 95, 119, 126, 138, 140, 206, 211, 212, 230, 234, 236, 245, 271, 310, 314, 322, 326, 353, 359.

Garth Blore: 39, 44, 126, 140, 338.
Reg Godwin: 368, 376, 377, 380.
Ed Roman: 10, 15.
Guy MacKenzie: 331.
Bob Greaves: 294.
Abel Guitars: 9
Aria Guitars: 18, 19
Art and Lutherie Guitars 20.
Barker Guitars: 26.
BC Glass Studios: 26.
Beyond the Trees: 31.
Blackbird Guitars: 33.
Blackspot Guitars: 34.
Breedlove Guitars: 39.
Burns Guitars: 42.
Bunker Guitars: 41.
Campbell Guitars: 55.
Crimson Guitars: 54.
Daisy Rock Guitars: 59, 61.
DePinto Guitars: 68,69,71.
Kevin Deane Guitars: 66.
Doolin Guitars: 77.
Dramm Guitars: 78.
Brian Eastwood Guitars: 83.
Emerald Guitars: 86, 87.
Epiphone: 88, 89, 90.
Ernie Ball Guitars: 92.
Fender Musical Instruments Corp.: 99, 101, 102, 105, 106, 314,
Frameworks Instruments: 114.
Framus Guitars: 115.
G&L Guitars: 112.
Godin Guitars: 143, 144.
Goldbug Guitars: 147.
Goldtone Guitars: 149.
Goulding Guitars: 152, 153.
Greenfield Guitars: 154, 157.
Gretsch Instruments: 157, 158, 159,160.
Guild Instruments: 166, 168, 162.
Guyatone: 170.
Hohner: 182.
Hutchins Guitars: 185.
Kay Guitars: 200.
Little Guitar Works: 221.
Luna Guitars: 225, 226.
Malden Guitars: 231, 232.
Modulus Guitars: 247, 248.
Monson Guitars: 248.
Novax Guitars: 258, 259.
Optek Guitars: 260.
Parker Guitars: 268, 272.
Prestige Guitars: 278, 279.
Rhinehart Guitars: 286.
Rim Custom Guitars: 290.
Roadrunner Guitars: 291.
Robin Guitars: 292.
Royale guitars: 294.
Saint Blues Guitars: 298.
Sigmund Guitars: 308.
Squier Guitars: 312.
Strobel Guitars: 325.
Takamine Guitars: 334.
Rick Toone Guitars: 342, 343.
Wal Custom Guitars: 362.
Washburn Guitars: 364, 366, 367, 374, 375,
Wendler Guitars: 371.
Wishbass: 378.
Xox Guitars: 384.
Zemaitis: 393, 395.
Zerberus: 394.
Every effort has been made to contact the copyright holders for images reproduced in this book.
Any omissions are entirely unintentional, and the details should be addressed to Quantum Publishing.

INDEX